Daniel
and
Revelation

A Study of Two Extraordinary Visions

James M. Efird

Wipf and Stock Publishers
EUGENE, OREGON

For My Wife

VIVIAN

who has shown me that love

can exist in this world

Wipf and Stock Publishers
199 West 8th Avenue, Suite 3
Eugene, Oregon 97401

Daniel and Revelation
A Study of Two Extraordinary Visions
By Efird, James M.
Copyright©1980 Efird, James M.
ISBN: 1-57910-674-9
Publication date: June, 2001
Previously published by Judson Press, Valley Forge, 1980.

Preface

Of all the books of the Bible there are two which stand out as the most difficult and intriguing to interpret—Daniel and Revelation. They also are the two books which fall into the literary category known as "apocalyptic." Apocalyptic literature seems strange to our minds, so much so that most people react in one of two ways when they encounter these mysterious biblical books: (1) some simply leave the books alone as utterly impossible to understand; (2) others become so preoccupied with them that they are convinced that the answers to the wide-ranging puzzles of the universe are somehow incorporated into and hidden within the strange and unusual images in these books. Too often those who follow the latter course become almost obsessed with the importance of these books and, possessed of a particular type of approach and interpretation, find ideas and schemes in the writings which were never intended.

Very often the problems that lay persons have in attempting to understand any of the books of the Bible are a result of the fact that they are not made aware that the Bible is a collection of different types of literature. If one chooses to read and study an English literature anthology, it is of great importance to know what kind of literature is being examined. People do not interpret poetry in the same way they do essays (and even essays differ in type and style), or essays the same way as drama, or drama the same way as fiction, or fiction the same way as history. The point is that in order to interpret properly any writing, something must be known about the kind of literature which is being used to transmit the writer's message and meaning.

The same approach is exceedingly helpful and also quite necessary to the person who wishes to study the books of the Bible. There are thirty-nine books of the Old Testament and twenty-seven books in the New Testament, and each one reflects a particular literary type and style. Knowing what kind of literature a particular book of the Bible reflects, therefore, is essential to a correct interpretation and understanding of the message of the book.

It is the purpose of this book to introduce the lay person to the literary type known as apocalyptic, to describe the characteristics of this kind of writing, and to give an interpretation of the books of Daniel and Revelation in accordance with that literary type. I shall also attempt to suggest ways in which the religious teachings of these books can be applicable to living in our "modern" society.

The author urges the reader to put aside at the very beginning everything which, up to this time, has been heard, read, or thought about the books of Daniel and Revelation and seek to understand each book and each message against the backdrop of its original historical setting. It is very important to follow this procedure because apocalyptic literature is so different from any literary genre with which most of us are familiar. In addition, most of what we have heard about these books has come from those who attempt to make of them something which they are not. i.e., timetables for the end of the world. It is also important that one read each book at a single sitting, *in toto,* and do this several times. The uncomfortable feeling of not really understanding will linger for a while, but when one begins to "get the feel" of this kind of writing, the reward will certainly be worth the effort!

Contents

Introduction

This world is not the best of all possible places to be. Even though there are marvels of science and technology which increase every day, giving to some a life of ease and a semblance of progress in human history, in the last analysis the earth has been and still is permeated by unspeakable evil. Even those whose lives, materially speaking, are easy and free from want are subject to forces of personal and impersonal evil which threaten to make insignificant and pitiful wretches of us all.

Sometimes this evil seems almost human because we experience it through human agencies. In these most enlightened times we still read about human selfishness, prejudice, and hatred which in extreme forms lead to unspeakable torture, genocide, starvation, and the like. These things are caused by human depravity either directly or indirectly.

At other points it appears that evil is an impersonal force which invades our world from the outside, that it is a horrible, faceless power against which it seems impossible to fight since we do not know whence it comes. Even if we knew its origin, we would not know how to combat it. There do seem to be, therefore, forces in this universe that go beyond our ability as human beings with human intelligence to comprehend and which threaten to overwhelm our world and our lives completely.

As difficult as it is to struggle against these two manifestations of evil separately, it is even more frightening when we remember that there are certain specific moments, certain particular situations in human history when these two forces of evil seem to combine and with their hideous and horrible strength seem intent on doing away with the last vestiges of human hope and decency. That is, there are times when it seems that these two forces of evil have combined in an intense effort to destroy those who have attempted to ally themselves with the forces of good, those who attempt to be the people of God. For persons who are experiencing such a moment of history, it seems that the forces of hell have taken complete and firm control of the earth and their lives.

It was in precisely such periods that the books of Daniel and Revelation were written. These two peculiar writings which are mysteries to most people in the twentieth century belong to a particular type of literary genre known as "apocalyptic." In order to understand these works filled with numbers, visions of beasts and dragons, and horrible scenes of evil and suffering, one must first of all seek to understand what kind of literature is being utilized to relay the message. Then he or she will be ready to ascertain exactly what kind of message is being relayed.

The type of literature which made extensive use of symbols and images usually surfaced in times of intense evil which inflicted suffering on those who attempted to stay on the path of good, justice, and truth. To these people, the age in which they lived was hopelessly corrupt and beyond redemption. The only hope which could be anticipated was an act of God by which the evil perpetrators of persecution would be destroyed. This act would then lead to a new age in which the persecution would be gone. These ideas were depicted by means of exaggerated figures, symbols, and images. So intense an evil as these people were experiencing could only be expressed appropriately by means of such symbolism. The destruction of this kind of evil, therefore, had to be described in even greater dimensions. The figures were huge and gigantic but the message was exceedingly simple, so simple that many if not most persons through the years have misunderstood these writings. The message was that God was in control of the created order no matter how it may have seemed at the moment. Evil would be destroyed by God. The persecution would *soon* be over; so the writer's message was to "keep the faith" even in the face of death itself. There were values in life which transcended the suffering of the moment.

The simplicity of the message coupled with the magnitude of the symbolism, therefore, have caused most persons to look for hidden meanings which were never really intended by the original writers. Because of this, unfortunately, apocalyptic books throughout the centuries have spawned wild notions about the end of the world. The history of the church is littered with the bleached bones of those who were certain that they had deciphered the mysteries of these books and could, therefore, predict the end of the world and the precise sequence of events leading up to that stupendous finish. Because of this and because of the wild claims made even today by those who follow in this long line of sincere but uninformed people, most persons shun the study of these two books, thereby missing a great message of comfort and strength for living in this world.

This is exceedingly regrettable; our world is so filled with evil in so many different forms and manifestations—evil which dehumanizes individuals and makes life quite painful—that it sometimes seems futile even to attempt any struggle against the powerful forces and institutions of this or any other era. It is not by accident that the books of Daniel and Revelation become popular in times of war and periods of alienation. Witness the flurry of commentaries and collections of sermons on these books which came from the periods of World War I and World War II. Note as well the intense interest in apocalyptic literature that has developed over the past decade or so in the face of the dehumanization process that so many feel from institutions, even the church, that have become too large and too impersonal.

Anytime, anywhere that people are faced with horrible and hideous evil which threatens to extinguish life, especially when persons are at least nominally dedicated to doing what is good and proper and right, the message of these two books should find a receptive audience. They contain a basic message of hope and a challenge to remain faithful to God even at the risk of the loss of all that is, humanly speaking, most dear and precious!

The following analysis of apocalyptic literature, its characteristics and message, will be followed by an exposition of the books of Daniel and Revelation. It is hoped that the reader will then be open to these great messages of strength and hope and faith which can sustain one even in the midst of the worst that the forces of evil can use against the people of God—then or now!

The Characteristics of Apocalyptic Literature

The word "apocalyptic" is an English derivative from a Greek word meaning "revelation" or "uncovering." This term is used to designate a particular kind of thought pattern which came into the religious development of the Jewish people sometime during the postexilic period (after 539 B.C.), primarily from the Persians. In the Zoroastrian religion of the Persians it was believed that there was in the universe a constant and mortal struggle being waged between the forces of good and the forces of evil, both of which had existed since the beginning. This struggle would someday eventuate in a climactic battle wherein the forces of good or light would defeat the forces of evil or darkness. This conflict would then bring history, as we understand it, to a close. Until that time, however, the battle would rage, and the world of humankind would be caught up in it; while evil had the upper hand, the people who had allied themselves with the good or light would suffer.

When these ideas came over into the religion of Israel, they were modified and altered in accordance with the Jewish understanding of Yahweh, their God. For example, the dualism of the Persians, understood as eternal, was changed. Good was viewed as eternal, but in Jewish apocalyptic thought evil was not eternal since it was not a part of the original order of creation but was rather an interloper. (Some refer to this type of thinking as "ethical" rather than "metaphysical" dualism.) Even so, the struggle between good and evil even in Jewish thought was being waged at a cosmic, spiritual level with each group having a leader and a group of helpers. This concept provided the impetus for the development in Jewish thought of the concept of angels and demons. And further, since the forces of good had a leader, namely God, the forces of evil were supplied with one in the figure of Satan (other names were also used for this epitome of evil in certain noncanonical works).

Whatever the characters, the struggle was one of life and death, and there was no escape from the battle or from choosing sides in the conflict, since the cosmic battle had concrete manifestations in the affairs of human history. This led, in Jewish apocalyptic thinking, to the idea of "two ages." The forces of evil were strong and aggressive and, for the time being, had control of human history. During this period evil flourished, which meant that those who had chosen right were subject to the whims of those evil persons who temporarily were in control. (This kind of setting immediately indicates that the period of human history in which this type of literature will flourish is a time of persecution.) The people of God, however, did not need to fear these evil times. Since the basic struggle was being waged at a level higher than the human level, the outcome would be decided at a level higher than the human. But because the battle was partially waged in this world, the results of the outcome would be manifested in this world order as well, meaning that the end of the persecution would definitely come, and *soon!*

This leads to a second emphasis in apocalyptic literature, namely the emphasis on "eschatology." Eschatology basically means "a study of the end"; "end," however, can have various connotations. The word in English usage may mean the end of an hour, the end of a class, the end of a period in one's life, the end of an era, or the end of everything. In Persian thought it meant the end of the historical process as humanly understood. But in the transfer to Jewish thought it primarily designated the end of an "age" or, in the context of the times in which it was written, the end of that particular age of persecution being experienced by the people of God. Whether this "end of the age" was thought to be identical to the end of history or the end of the world is debatable, for each apocalyptic writer had the freedom to interpret these matters as he wished. And at this time there was little consistency in their thinking about the end of the world if, truly, there would be such an end. Therefore each apocalyptic writing (and there were many which were not included in the canons of the Old and New Testaments) must be examined carefully to determine what kind of teaching about the "end" is intended by the author. Whatever else is meant, however, the basic idea is that there is a present age under the influence and dominion of the forces of evil. This evil will increase, and, therefore, suffering by the people of God will accordingly increase, until evil "runs its course," at which time God will intervene on behalf of his people, destroy the evil, and remove the persecution. A new age will then be inaugurated in which the people of God will be able to worship as they should and live in peace, free from persecution. Some noncanonical apocalyptic works do seem to teach that the end of the age of persecution is synonymous with the end of this world order. Upon close examination, however, it is clear that the two biblical apocalyptic works do *not* see an end to history or this world order as we know it. Both conclude with a positive outlook on the created order and history. Both teach basically that the end of the persecution will come *soon* and that God's people will then be able to worship him freely within this historical process. God has and always will triumph over evil.

Because evil is so strong and powerful and persecution so vicious and ugly, their portraits must be painted in grotesque and horrible dimensions. And, because evil is so grotesque, its fall and the one who causes its fall must be depicted in even greater dimensions that stagger the imagination. Therefore, apocalyptic literature developed an elaborate system of symbolism and imagery. This symbolism is one of the chief characteristics of this particular literary genre. And it is precisely here that so many persons fail to recognize that in essence apocalyptic literature is poetry written in prose, and that this kind of poet must be allowed not only the usual "poetic license" but also the freedom of an immense imagination.

One recent commentator on the book of Revelation compares the imagery of apocalyptic literature with our contemporary political cartoons.[1] This is an appropriate analogy. If, for example, one had seen, after the presidential election of 1976, a political cartoon of a giant peanut with a large toothy smile standing with its foot on a world globe, there would be no question as to its meaning. We understand this because it is a part of our culture. If, however, someone several centuries from now were to find this cartoon and interpret it as a sign of the end of the world and would postulate from that cartoon that the evil enemy was the group of peanut-growing countries of the earth banding together to take over the world, we would know that this was an illegitimate use of the material. Something quite similar to this, unfortunately, has too often happened with apocalyptic imagery. The meaning of the symbol in its original setting has been ignored and thereby misunderstood.

Another example could be drawn from the book known as IV Ezra (sometimes known also as II Esdras), an apocalyptic writing found among the apocryphal books. Here the reader is introduced to a vision in which there is a great eagle flying in mid-air. It is to be destroyed because it has persecuted the people of God. In its

[1] G. R. Beasley-Murray, *The Book of Revelation* (Greenwood, S.C.: The Attic Press, 1974), pp. 16-17.

historical setting the eagle represents Rome which had just recently crushed the Jewish people in the A.D. 66—70 war between the two adversaries. The author was saying that God would judge Rome because that nation had inflicted evil on the people of God. For someone today to interpret this as a prediction that the United States (whose symbol today is the eagle) is the evil persecutor of God's people and that the end of the world will come with the judgment on the United States would be sheer speculative hypothesis and fanciful imagination based neither on fact nor on historical reality.

One should always keep in mind that symbols and images used by the apocalyptic writers were meant to convey meaning. They were not intended to depict (or predict) literal events or scenes—as in a photograph—but rather were meant to be "seen" impressionistically as one must see a giant mural which overwhelms the viewer with its greatness and message. In such a mural some details may be important in themselves, but most take on meaning only in the context of the larger scene. It is the totality of the picture that is meant to convey meaning.

These apocalyptic murals, then, were painted by means of elaborate symbolism. Some of the major symbols and images utilized by these writers have a degree of consistency about them, but in some instances the author must simply be followed in his use of the symbol. One of the major ways symbolism was used was in the device of visions where the writer (usually some ancient worthy of the past, such as Ezra, Baruch, or Abraham) "saw" a vision complete with all kinds of images which he did not understand. These images were generally in the form of beasts, grotesque and weird, sometimes even composites of various species. Usually these stood for empires or kings. Horns were often attached to the beasts; these horns usually represented kings or simply the power which a ruler exercised. These great and unusual scenes which appeared before the "seer" caused much consternation; the person was completely befuddled as to the meaning of the things he had just seen. Another typical apocalyptic device used an angel as a guide to the person seeing the vision; at the conclusion, the angel explained to the seer the meaning of the events depicted.

It is often argued that apocalyptic literature is cryptic and that the authors used this type of weird symbolism in order that the ones who were persecuting the people of God would not understand what was being said. This seems very unlikely, however, especially when these visions are explained in clear and uncomplicated language (see Daniel 8:18-26 and Revelation 17:9-18). It is more likely that the perpetrators of the persecution were unconcerned about what these people were writing. To them these "tracts" were idealistic and unrealistic musings of a people who had no power; what harm could such hopes do when they, the powerful, held the captives in bondage? It would hurt nothing for them to write such documents; they may have even thought them a help, keeping the oppressed happy in their misery. Our conclusion, therefore, is that the exaggerated symbolism utilized in this type of literature had as its purpose not an attempt to hide the message from the persecutor but rather to encourage faith on the part of the persecuted. The reason for this was that this literature with its utilization of extreme symbols and images was tailor-made for such a purpose, and through the exaggerated symbolism something of the dimensions and importance of what was happening could be depicted.

One of the chief symbolic devices is the use of numbers. Most persons are superstitious about numbers, but in the ancient world it was thought that certain numbers had meaning and power in themselves! The apocalyptic writers made extensive use of number symbolism. Generally speaking, "three" in apocalyptic writing is the number used to designate the "spirit" world, and "four" to denote the created order. "Seven" is the number of perfection (or sometimes completeness). The number "ten" is used quite frequently to designate totality, while "twelve" denotes the people of God (in Jewish and Christian apocalypses). Not only can numbers be used alone to convey certain ideas, but they also are used together and often in terms of multiples. For example, the number 1,000 represents completeness raised to an even higher level. The famous figure of 144,000 is simply 10^3 times 12^2, the complete number (10) raised to an even fuller designation and the number symbolizing the people of God (12) increased as well. The resulting figure is simply symbolic of the magnitude of the total number of the people of God.

One other number should be mentioned, namely "three and one-half." (This is also represented as 42 months or 1,260 days.) "Three and one-half" is almost always associated with the time that evil is allowed to work its destruction and cause the elect of God to suffer. Whether this is because its value is half of seven, the total or perfect number, and thus symbolizes the belief that evil will run its course but is not eternal, or whether it reflects some historical event lost to our investigations is a matter of little importance here. That it does symbolize the passing and finite limits of the exercise and domination of evil is clear enough.

Colors are also used to represent certain ideas or values. White, which is used most frequently, normally designates victory or conquering. (It is very seldom that it denotes purity.) Red is usually connected with war or strife while black represents hard times, especially the periods of famine and pestilence which can follow war. In the book of Revelation "pale" or "greenish-gray" denotes death, since this is the color of a corpse. Other colors are also used but without any real pattern of meaning, even though green may denote eternity. As with the apocalyptic writers' use of precious gems in describing a scene, often the color simply adds to the stupendous, overwhelming nature of the spectacle.

In studying apocalyptic literature, if the reader will attempt to think in terms of symbols and their meaning instead of literal figures, the first step will have been made toward understanding how to interpret this type of writing. For example, when one reads 10 (or a multiple of 10), one should think "completeness" or "totality" rather than 10 *per se*. When one reads the number 12 (or a multiple of 12), one should think "relating to the people of God." These kinds of matters will be pointed out explicitly in the exposition of the books of Daniel and Revelation which will follow shortly.

Two other characteristics of apocalyptic writings are pessimism and determinism. The pessimistic outlook of the writer is, of course, a result of the fact of persecution. The pessimism was related to the contemporary evil age, however, not to the entire historical process, for the writer's age was under the dominion of evil which had to be removed before the better age could be enjoyed. Since the real writer was usually pseudonymous and designated himself as some ancient worthy of the past, there was an historical section in almost every apocalyptic work depicting history by means of a progression of events in symbolic form. The purpose of this seems to be not simply to recite history showing how the present situation of persecution evolved, but to encourage the people under the persecution. This could be done by showing that the events of the past (*predicted* in terms of the ancient worthy) had in fact come to pass. If these events and the suffering had occurred as predicted (i.e., determined), would not the destruction of evil come about as predicted as well?

It must be remembered that the apocalyptic author was always writing in a situation where there was persecution, a hideous aberration of human sin already hideous enough. The duty, then, of the writer was to use every means possible to bolster the faith of the persecuted people. When the present is unbearable, one always looks to the future. And such a situation makes one think about the possibilities of human life—and death—especially when death comes to good people at the hands of vicious and evil people.

It was at the impetus of the apocalyptic writers that a doctrine of life after death in Jewish thought really developed. Up to this time the concept of Sheol prevailed. Sheol was a place of gloom and darkness where everyone, rich or poor, good or bad, slave or free, went upon physical death. The Old Testament did not have a concept of annihilation; the life in Sheol was, however, the weakest kind of life one could imagine. There were no rewards or punishments in Sheol, only a gloomy, barely distinguishable existence. Most Old Testament religious thinking held that rewards or punishments were meted out in this life; however, under the cruel realities of real life and especially in times of persecution such as these, it became obvious that the world was not always structured that way. Therefore in this period (200 B.C.—A.D. 100) there were many persons, especially the apocalyptic writers, who wrestled with a concept of life after death which provided for some kind of reward and/or punishment. After all, if a person were martyred, some procedure had to be devised so that that kind of faith could be rewarded; and further, that some kind of appropriate action had to be taken to deal with that kind of evil.

It would be easy to relegate these apocalyptic writers to the realm of wishful thinkers who said what they could to the people who were suffering—it would be easy to charge that they simply "wished" there were some kind of hope for suffering people. Such a writer's thought might be: "give any kind of hope even if it is false hope"—but this would miss the point entirely. The Jewish people believed in a God of justice and righteousness as well as mercy, and it was from the basic understanding of the nature of their God that the essential elements in apocalyptic writing developed. It was because God was powerful over all things and the Ruler of history that the writers would give assurance to the people. It was because he was just and righteous that they believed evil would be destroyed—not simply because they wished it! It was because he was a God who kept his promises that they could believe, in spite of even the most extreme acts of cruelty against his people, that he would make certain that they (each group!) received their rightful reward. The great hope of the apocalyptic writers lay in the nature of the God they worshiped and to whom they had committed their lives.

The Book of Daniel

Background

In order to understand any literary work, it is necessary to know as much as can be known about the historical setting out of which the writing emerged. This is even more true of an apocalyptic work since a knowledge of the historical setting is essential for the proper understanding of any apocalyptic writing. The age in which the writers lived, even though it was evil, was very important to their message; how their particular situation had emerged from the past was an integral part of the writers' schemes.

Most persons are aware of the great military conquests of the Macedonian, Alexander the Great. With dreams of a world empire unified by allegiance to him as king (and god?) and a blend of Oriental and Greek cultures (called Hellenistic), Alexander swept over much of the world known in his era of history. In his conquests he encouraged intermarriage of Greek soldiers with the people whom they had conquered, established Greek cities, and encouraged the adoption of the Greek language, customs, and philosophies. This was a process called *Hellenization.*

Alexander died suddenly in 323 B.C. When this happened, his generals began to fight among themselves for possession of the territories won by the triumphs of their leader. These wars are called the Wars of the Diadochi (successors). When the smoke of the battles had cleared (around 301 B.C.), the empire had been divided into four sections. Two of the divisions need not detain us here. The other two, however, had a direct bearing on the history of the Jewish people and the subsequent setting for the book of Daniel. Egypt and southern Palestine were under the control of Ptolemy, while northern Palestine and the old Persian empire were controlled by Seleucus.

The place where the Jews lived was especially contested, since it lay in the area between the Ptolemaic kingdom in Egypt and the Seleucid kingdom to the north and east. Even though the territory was something of a battleground in a tug-of-war, the Jews were nominally, at least, under the control of Egypt. The Ptolemies were not very concerned with the process of Hellenization; so, therefore, the Jews were left alone, for the most part, as far as their religious beliefs and practices were concerned. The Seleucids, on the other hand, were much more aggressive in their zeal for pressing the Hellenization process.

Many battles continued to be fought over the disputed land, until finally in 198 B.C. the Egyptians were defeated at Panium (or Banias) at which time they abandoned any further hope of retaining the territory. The rule then passed to the Seleucids. Economically, the area was exceedingly poor. The Egyptians exacted very little in terms of taxation; and when the Seleucids took over, Antiochus III (king of the Seleucid empire) decided that Judah would not have to pay any taxes for a period of three years. The situation must have been exceedingly bad!

The tiny country of Judah was governed by the high priest; the Jews did not really separate religion from affairs of state. The high priest was to be a descendant of Aaron. The office of high priest had to be at least confirmed by the ruling overlords since the high priest exercised not only religious but also political rule. In 175 B.C. when Antiochus IV became king, a certain Joshua who was brother of the current high priest, Onias III, bribed the Syrian ruler and had himself appointed high priest in place of his brother! This caused a tense situation among the Jewish people which was intensified because Joshua pursued the Hellenization policies of the Seleucids. Greek ideas and customs were encouraged. Joshua even changed his name to Jason, the Greek equivalent! In 171 B.C. a certain person who was *not* of the priestly family offered a larger bribe to Antiochus for the office of high priest. Not one to allow an opportunity to pass by, Antiochus accepted and appointed Menelaus (sometimes called Menahem) to the office. The Jewish people, outraged before, were now furious; and when a false rumor about the death of Antiochus spread (in approximately 169 B.C.), Jason led a rebellion against Menelaus and assumed the office again. But the reports of Antiochus's death (like Mark Twain's) were exaggerated. He returned and established Menelaus in the office and plundered the temple. The situation was tense indeed, since some of the Jews did accept the Hellenization policies. Strife and unrest continued until Antiochus, realizing that the basic problem lay in the religion of these people, proscribed Judaism. It was termed a capital offense to worship as Jews, to have a copy of the Torah, or to circumcise one's children. A statue of Zeus was erected in the temple, and a pig was sacrificed on the altar there!

In 168–167 B.C. at a small village called Modein, an old priest and his sons triggered the opposition by killing a Syrian officer and fleeing to the mountains to wage guerrilla warfare against these oppressors. The old priest's name was Mattathias; he died shortly after the fighting began, but his son Judas (called Maccabeus) continued the struggle. In 165–164 Judas defeated the Syrians in a battle, the outcome of which lifted the proscription against Judaism. Many persons who had joined in the fight for religious freedom were then content to stop, but Judas and his followers continued to fight for political independence, and by 141 B.C. had won a measure of it. The details of that struggle, however, are not relevant to our study.

It was in this setting, 168–165 B.C., that the author of the book of Daniel wrote. The people of God who were attempting to keep the religious law were forbidden to do so under pain of death. In fact, they were actually required to worship in other ways. In the midst of this kind of situation the author of Daniel writes to encourage the people to "keep the faith!"

The dating of an apocalyptic work is sometimes very difficult. This is because of the symbolic presentation of history which the authors use, because of the fact that apocalyptic writers are quite free in appropriating materials from other times and circumstances for their own works, and because of our own lack of knowledge of the detailed history of the period under consideration. Usually the work can be dated, however, by a close examination of the symbolic historical panorama included somewhere in the writing. When the facts as we know them cease to be accurate and subsequent events are misrepresented in detail, the reader can generally date the book fairly closely. For example, in Daniel we find history moving along in accord with what we know about the times. But suddenly the facts as we know them differ from the scenes as depicted by the apocalyptic writer. In this book the author depicted the death of Antiochus IV at one time and place, when in reality he died in another time and place. (This will be dealt with in detail at the appropriate place in the text, 11:40-45.) Therefore most scholars feel that since Antiochus actually did die in 164 B.C., the book of Daniel was written just before the ban of proscription was lifted, i.e., sometime before mid-165.

The book itself consists of twelve chapters divided almost evenly into two sections, chapters 1-6 and chapters 7-12. The first section is really not apocalyptic *per se* but consists of delightful stories about certain Jewish youths who found themselves in exile in Babylon. These stories, however, spoke directly to the points at issue during the persecution under Antiochus, and they are quite similar to other books and stories popular at the time—for instance, Tobit and Judith of the Apocrypha. Chapters 7-12 are apocalyptic, however, and reflect all the typical apocalyptic characteristics. These sections will be commented on in detail at the appropriate place in the exposition of the texts.

There is one curious point about which the reader should be aware even though it has nothing to do with the interpretation of the book. This curious phenomenon is that the book is written in two languages, Hebrew and Aramaic; and these languages do not correspond to the two basic sections but rather overlap. The book begins in Hebrew, 1:1-2:4a; but beginning with 2:4b and continuing through 7:28 the text is written in Aramaic. At that point the text reverts to Hebrew and remains in that language through the conclusion of the book. Scholars argue over the reasons for the language division and the truth must be guessed at; in all probability the situation has to do with the fact that the author probably used the stories (chapters 1-6) which were written in Aramaic and combined them with his own apocalyptic visions in Hebrew. He then translated the beginning of the initial section into Hebrew and the beginning of the apocalyptic section into Aramaic to give a greater semblance of unity to the two sections. This is an interesting feature of the book, critically speaking, but, as has been indicated, it has nothing to do with the interpretation of the book and its message.

One further motif must be discussed before we turn to the text itself. There are many who place the book of Daniel among the prophets and classify it as a "prophecy," usually meaning a "foretelling" of something in the future. It is easy to understand how this misunderstanding could take place, since the order of our Old Testament books seems to follow a chronological sequence, and, chronologically speaking, Daniel follows Ezekiel. Our order, however, is derived from the order of the Septuagint, the Greek translation of the Old Testament, through the Latin Vulgate; but in the Hebrew canon of the Old Testament, the books are divided into three sections, the Law (Torah, Hebrew), the Prophets (Nebiim, Hebrew), and the Writings (Kethubim, Hebrew). The book of Daniel is not included among the prophets, but it is found in the third and latest group of the Old Testament canon. That there are elements of prediction in the book of Daniel is without doubt. And that these elements share a certain amount of similarity with certain aspects of the prophetic thought is not to be denied either. But the fact is that Daniel is not a prophetic writing and was not intended to be even though it may at points contain certain ideas and motifs that one could call "prophetic."

Exposition

Chapter 1—Keeping the Faith by Observing the Food Laws

Verses 1-2: In the third year of the reign of Jehoiakim king of Judah, Nebuchadnezzar king of Babylon came to Jerusalem and besieged it. And the Lord gave Jehoiakim king of Judah into his hand, with some of the vessels of the house of God; and he brought them to the land of Shinar, to the house of his god, and placed the vessels in the treasury of his god.

The first verse gives an historical setting to the book. The fact that the date is incorrect does not alter the meaning of the story in any way. The third year of Jehoiakim was 606 B.C., but we know that Nebuchadnezzar did not first carry away captives until 598-597. The practice of taking precious valuables from the conquered peoples' temple and placing them in the temple of the god of the captor was a common practice in those days. It is interesting that the author used the term "Shinar" for Babylon. This is not unique with him; it is a matter of some interest that Zechariah (5:5-11) depicts the banishment of wickedness from the Holy Land to Shinar. The designation of Babylon here may have been the author's way of saying to his readers that these people whose stories are about to be told were in the midst of a hostile and evil enemy.

Verses 3-7: Then the king commanded Ashpenaz, his chief eunuch, to bring some of the people of Israel, both of the royal family and of the nobility, youths without blemish, handsome and skilful in all wisdom, endowed with knowledge, understanding learning, and competent to serve in the king's palace, and to teach them the letters and language of the Chaldeans. The king assigned them a daily portion of the rich food which the king ate, and of the wine which he drank. They were to be educated for three years, and at the end of that time they were to stand before the king. Among these were Daniel, Hananiah, Mishael, and Azariah of the tribe of Judah. And the chief of the eunuchs gave them names: Daniel he called Belteshazzar, Hananiah he called Shadrach, Mishael he called Meshach, and Azariah he called Abednego.

Again, it was not uncommon for captors to train and use gifted captives in their service. These persons were to be trained for three years. Included in this training were the spoils of being treated well in the court at the king's expense, something which would speak to the self-interests of most persons. But the food of the king's table was not *kosher;* it violated the Jewish food laws. Therefore to refuse to eat of this food was not a matter of health but of religious conviction. This was one of the pressing issues facing the Jewish people at this time under Antiochus's proscription. That this issue should have had such significance is surprising, but the fact is that it did. One can read about this aspect of postexilic Judaism in many of the so-called intertestamental writings (the *Apocrypha* and *Pseudepigrapha* of the Old Testament). One instance in particular could be cited as an illustration since it comes from this very period of Antiochus's persecution and is found in II Maccabees 7. Here we have a story about a woman and her seven sons who were martyred in horrible fashion because they refused to eat religiously unclean food.

It is interesting that in verse 6 we are given the Hebrew names for these young men and in verse 7 the names which the Babylonians gave to them. There may be some significance here because many persons were changing their names to Greek equivalents in the Hellenizing process after 175 B.C. The fact that Daniel was called by his Hebrew name throughout the book and the other three by both their Hebrew and their Babylonian names may reflect a feeling on the part of the author that the change of names meant little one way or the other. Name changes were not at issue; basic religious beliefs and identity were.

Verses 8-16: But Daniel resolved that he would not defile himself with the king's rich food, or with the wine which he drank; therefore he asked the chief of the eunuchs to allow him not to defile himself. And God gave Daniel favor and compassion in the sight of the chief of the eunuchs; and the chief of the eunuchs said to Daniel, "I fear lest my lord the king, who appointed your food and your drink, should see that you were in poorer condition than the youths who are of your own age. So you would endanger my head with the king." Then Daniel said to the steward whom the chief of the eunuchs had appointed over Daniel, Hananiah, Mishael, and Azariah; "Test your servants for ten days; let us be given vegetables to eat and water to drink. Then let our appearance and the appearance of the youths who eat the king's rich food be observed by you, and according to what you see deal with your servants." So he hearkened to them in this matter, and tested them for ten days.

At the end of ten days it was seen that they were better in appearance and fatter in flesh than all the youths who ate the king's rich food. So the steward took away their rich food and the wine they were to drink, and gave them vegetables.

Daniel resolved not to eat foods that were religiously unclean. He appealed to those in authority to allow a test. They should let the others eat the king's food; he and his friends would eat their own food. The outcome would decide the issue (verse 13). At the end of the ten days (a completed period of time) the Jewish youths were found to be much better in appearance than all the others who had eaten the king's food. Therefore all the youths were given what Daniel and his friends had eaten!

Verses 17-21: As for these four youths, God gave them learning and skill in all letters and wisdom; and Daniel had understanding in all visions and dreams. At the end of the time, when the king had commanded that they should be brought in, the chief of the eunuchs brought them in before Nebuchadnezzar. And the king spoke with them, and among them all none was found like Daniel, Hananiah, Mishael, and Azariah; therefore they stood before the king. And in every matter of wisdom and understanding concerning which the king inquired of them, he found them ten times better than all the magicians and enchanters that were in all his kingdom. And Daniel continued until the first year of King Cyrus.

God caused Daniel and his three friends to excel in the training which they had been given. It is interesting to note that Daniel was also given understanding in visions and dreams; this prepares the reader for some of the episodes to follow. The four impressed the king and were found to be "ten times better than all the magicians and enchanters" in the kingdom. The chapter concludes with the statement that Daniel remained until the first year of Cyrus. Whether this reference had some significance in terms of Cyrus's being the one who defeated the Babylonians and allowed the Jews to return to Palestine, or whether it simply was a reference to the fact that Daniel survived and worked for the Chaldeans in an official capacity as long as they were in power, or whether there was some other reason, we do not know precisely.

Summary

The first chapter sets the stage for the remainder of the book.

Daniel and his friends were introduced; they found favor in the land and in the court in spite of (or because of) their insistence on retaining their identity as Jews. They continued to be loyal to their God, but they did not totally reject working for and with the Chaldeans in a new setting, nor did they mind being given new names. It may be that the author, while his basic purpose remained to encourage persons in keeping the religious heritage pure, intended also to encourage an openness to new culture and customs. Working with the Chaldeans proved to be in this story an example of how one could demonstrate that certain aspects of one's own religion and culture may be desirable enough to persuade others to adopt them!

Questions for Further Consideration

1. What kinds of situations today place persons in positions in which they are asked to compromise their religious heritage and convictions? Name as many as you can.

2. What is the answer to the kind of question which the author of Daniel suggests? How would we apply the principle to the specific situations you have given in question 1?

3. In keeping one's faith "pure," is it always necessary to reject all other culture and learning? Why or why not?

Chapter 2—Nebuchadnezzar's Dream of Four Empires

Verses 1-11: In the second year of the reign of Nebuchadnezzar, Nebuchadnezzar had dreams; and his spirit was troubled, and his sleep left him. Then the king commanded that the magicians, the enchanters, the sorcerers, and the Chaldeans be summoned, to tell the king his dreams. So they came in and stood before the king. And the king said to them, "I had a dream, and my spirit is troubled to know the dream." Then the Chaldeans said to the king, "O king, live for ever! Tell your servants the dream, and we will show the interpretation." The king answered the Chaldeans, "The word from me is sure: if you do not make known to me the dream and its interpretation, you shall be torn limb from limb, and your houses shall be laid in ruins. But if you show the dream and its interpretation, you shall receive from me gifts and rewards and great honor. Therefore show me the dream and its interpretation." They answered a second time, "Let the king tell his servants the dream, and we will show its interpretation." The king answered, "I know with certainty that you are trying to gain time, because you see that the word from me is sure that if you do not make the dream known to me, there is but one sentence for you. You have agreed to speak lying and corrupt words before me till the times change. Therefore tell me the dream, and I shall know that you can show me its interpretation." The Chaldeans answered the king, "There is not a man on earth who can meet the king's demand; for no great and powerful king has asked such a thing of any magician or enchanter or Chaldean. The thing that the king asks is difficult, and none can show it to the king except the gods, whose dwelling is not with flesh."

The story here is set within the reign of Nebuchadnezzar, king of Babylon, who had a dream and demanded that his corps of wise men and magicians tell him both the dream and its interpretation. His decree was such that if they were unable to do the feat, they would be destroyed. The key verse is verse 11; its sets the stage for the following scenes. "The thing that the king asks is hard, and none can show it to the king except the gods, whose dwelling is not with flesh."

Verses 12-24: Because of this the king was angry and very furious, and commanded that all the wise men of Babylon be destroyed. So the decree went forth that the wise men were to be slain, and they sought Daniel and his companions, to slay them. Then Daniel replied with prudence and discretion to Arioch, the captain of the king's guard, who had gone out to slay the wise men of Babylon; he said to Arioch, the king's captain, "Why is the decree of the king so severe?" Then Arioch made the matter known to Daniel. And Daniel went in and besought the king to appoint him a time, that he might show to the king the interpretation.

Then Daniel went to his house and made the matter known to Hananiah, Mishael, and Azariah, his companions, and told them to seek mercy of the God of heaven concerning this mystery, so that Daniel and his companions might not perish with the rest of the wise men of Babylon. Then the mystery was revealed to Daniel in a vision of the night. Then Daniel blessed the God of heaven. Daniel said:

> "Blessed be the name of God for
> ever and ever,
> to whom belong wisdom and might.
>
> He changes times and seasons;
> he removes kings and sets up kings;
> he gives wisdom to the wise
> and knowledge to those who have
> understanding;
> he reveals deep and mysterious things;
> he knows what is in the darkness,
> and the light dwells with him.
>
> To thee, O God of my fathers,
> I give thanks and praise,
> for thou hast given me wisdom and
> strength,
> and hast now made known to me
> what we asked of thee,
> for thou hast made known to us
> the king's matter."

Therefore Daniel went in to Arioch, whom the king had appointed to destroy the wise men of Babylon; he went and said thus to him, "Do not destroy the wise men of Babylon; bring me in before the king, and I will show the king the interpretation."

Since the dream had not been interpreted, the king gave the decree to destroy all the wise men of Babylon. Daniel and his friends were among those who were "rounded up." Daniel asked Arioch, the one who had been commissioned to carry out the order, about the matter and, when told, asked the king for an audience. Daniel and his three friends prayed about the matter, and, in a "vision of the night," the details were revealed to Daniel. He then asked Arioch not to carry out the order but to take him to the king.

> Verses 25-30: Then Arioch brought in Daniel before the king in haste, and said thus to him: "I have found among the exiles from Judah a man who can make known to the king the interpretation." The king said to Daniel, whose name was Belteshazzar, "Are you able to make known to me the dream that I have seen and its interpretation?" Daniel answered the king, "No wise men, enchanters, magicians, or astrologers can show to the king the mystery which the king has asked, but there is a God in heaven who reveals mysteries, and he has made known to King Nebuchadnezzar what will be in the latter days. Your dream and the visions of your head as you lay in bed are these: To you, O king, as you lay in bed came thoughts of what would be hereafter, and he who reveals mysteries made known to you what is to be. But as for me, not because of any wisdom that I have more than all the living has this mystery been revealed to me, but in order that the interpretation may be made known to the king, and that you may know the thoughts of your mind."

Daniel told the king that God had revealed to him (Nebuchadnezzar) the mysteries of the future. And that same God had revealed to him (Daniel) the interpretation of the vision.

> Verses 31-35: "You saw, O king, and behold, a great image. This image, mighty and of exceeding brightness, stood before you, and its appearance was frightening. The head of this image was of fine gold, its breast and arms of silver, and its belly and thighs of bronze, its legs of iron, its feet partly of iron and partly of clay. As you looked, a stone was cut out by no human hand, and it smote the image on its feet of iron and clay, and broke them in pieces; then the iron, the clay, the bronze, the silver, and the gold, all together were broken in pieces, and became like the chaff of the summer threshing floors; and the wind carried them away, so that not a trace of them could be found. But the stone that struck the image became a great mountain and filled the whole earth."

What the king had seen in his dream was a huge image with a head of fine gold, arms and breast of silver, belly and thighs of bronze, and legs of iron with the feet of iron mixed with clay. While he looked at the image, a stone "cut out by no human hand" shattered the image by striking its feet. Then the stone began to grow so that it became a great mountain that filled the earth.

Verses 36-45: "This was the dream; now we will tell the king its interpretation. You, O king, the king of kings, to whom the God of heaven has given the kingdom, the power, and the might, and the glory, and into whose hand he has given, wherever they dwell, the sons of men, the beasts of the field, and the birds of the air, making you rule over them all—you are the head of gold. After you shall arise another kingdom inferior to you, and yet a third kingdom of bronze, which shall rule over all the earth. And there shall be a fourth kingdom, strong as iron, because iron breaks to pieces and shatters all things; and like iron which crushes, it shall break and crush all these. And as you saw the feet and toes partly of potter's clay and partly of iron. it shall be a divided kingdom; but some of the firmness of iron shall be in it, just as you saw iron mixed with the miry clay. And as the toes of the feet were partly iron and partly clay, so the kingdom shall be partly strong and partly brittle. As you saw the iron mixed with miry clay, so they will mix with one another in marriage, but they will not hold together, just as iron does not mix with clay. And in the days of those kings the God of heaven will set up a kingdom which shall never be destroyed, nor shall its sovereignty be left to another people. It shall break in pieces all these kingdoms and bring them to an end, and it shall stand for ever; just as you saw that a stone was cut from a mountain by no human hand, and that it broke in pieces the iron, the bronze, the clay, the silver, and the gold. A great God has made known to the king what shall be hereafter. The dream is certain, and its interpretation sure."

Daniel then proceeded to explain to the king the interpretation of what he had seen in the dream. The solution to the riddle was that each of the parts of the image symbolized a human kingdom. The head of gold was Babylon. After that would come an inferior kingdom, the Median, and a third one that would rule over all the earth, Persia. The fourth, represented by the legs of iron and the feet of iron and clay, was Greece. The shattering and breaking characteristics of that kingdom symbolized Alexander the Great's swift and efficient victories in that part of the world. As we know, after Alexander's death his generals fought and ultimately divided the empire into four sections (see verses 41-43). The reference in verse 43 to "marriage" probably refers to marriages between the Seleucids and the Ptolemies which did not make for lasting alliances as they were supposed to do. Verse 44 indicates that in that time (i.e., the Maccabean era) God would intervene and establish his kingdom. The stone "cut [from the mountain] by no human hand" is representative of the kingdom of God.

> Verses 46-49: Then King Nebuchadnezzar fell upon his face, and did homage to Daniel, and commanded that an offering and incense be offered up to him. The king said to Daniel, "Truly, your God is God of gods and Lord of kings, and a revealer of mysteries, for you have been able to reveal this mystery." Then the king gave Daniel high honors and many great gifts, and made him ruler over the whole province of Babylon, and chief prefect over all the wise men of Babylon. Daniel made request of the king, and he appointed Shadrach, Meshach, and Abednego over the affairs of the province of Babylon; but Daniel remained at the king's court.

The paying of homage to Daniel and his subsequent promotion, along with that of his friends, is a typical postexilic motif indicating that soon all nations would honor Israel in this manner (see Isaiah 2:1-4; Micah 4; Zechariah 8:20-23; 14:16-21; Obadiah, v. 21; Joel 3:16-21).

Summary

This chapter is one that helps to provide unity for the book of Daniel. The vision here, while not thoroughly apocalyptic in every respect, nevertheless reflects apocalyptic tendencies and characteristics. Further, the meaning of this chapter is essentially the same as that of the apocalyptic vision in chapter 7. The chapter means to say to those people enduring persecution under Antiochus IV that the time is near for the intervention of God on behalf of his people. They could see from the symbolic representation that indeed, generally speaking, the course of history had come to pass as it was depicted here. If those other things had occurred, could God's help for them be far away?

Questions for Further Consideration

1. In the light of the historical context of the times in which Daniel was written, what present significance should be made of the dream of the king which depicted an historical sequence of nations?

    a) Is the important point here the specific identification of the four kingdoms?

    b) Or is it rather the identity of the kingdom or reign of God?

  2. Why would this historical recounting of the times be a source of hope and inspiration for the people to whom this book was addressed?

Chapter 3—Keeping the Faith by Refusing to Compromise

Verses 1-7: King Nebuchadnezzar made an image of gold, whose height was sixty cubits and its breadth six cubits. He set it up on the plain of Dura, in the province of Babylon. Then King Nebuchadnezzar sent to assemble the satraps, the prefects, and the governors, the counselors, the treasurers, the justices, the magistrates, and all the officials of the provinces to come to the dedication of the image which King Nebuchadnezzar had set up. Then the satraps, the prefects, and the governors, the counselors, the treasurers, the justices, the magistrates, and all the officials of the provinces, were assembled for the dedication of the image that King Nebuchadnezzar had set up; and they stood before the image that Nebuchadnezzar had set up. And the herald proclaimed aloud, "You are commanded, O peoples, nations, and languages, that when you hear the sound of the horn, pipe, lyre, trigon, harp, bagpipe, and every kind of music, you are to fall down and worship the golden image that King Nebuchadnezzar has set up; and whoever does not fall down and worship shall immediately be cast into a burning fiery furnace." Therefore, as soon as all the peoples heard the sound of the horn, pipe, lyre, trigon, harp, bagpipe, and every kind of music, all the peoples, nations, and languages fell down and worshiped the golden image which King Nebuchadnezzar had set up.

King Nebuchadnezzar caused a huge image to be made of gold (probably gold-plated), most likely of the god of the Babylonians. He ordered that all persons bow down and worship the image at the blast of musical sound. Anyone who refused to do this was to be executed by being thrown into a furnace of fire. Note the size of the statue: sixty cubits high (a cubit was about eighteen inches) and six cubits wide.

Verses 8-12: Therefore at that time certain Chaldeans came forward and maliciously accused the Jews. They said to King Nebuchadnezzar, "O king, live for ever! You, O king, have made a decree, that every man who hears the sound of the horn, pipe, lyre, trigon, harp, bagpipe, and every kind of music, shall fall down and worship the golden image; and whoever does not fall down and worship shall be cast into a burning fiery furnace. There are certain Jews whom you have appointed over the affairs of the province of Babylon: Shadrach, Meshach, and Abednego. These men, O king, pay no heed to you; they do not serve your gods or worship the golden image which you have set up."

There were some persons who knew about the three young Jews who did not worship the gods of the land and therefore did not worship the image. These people, probably to receive a reward for themselves, told the king about Shadrach, Meshach, and Abednego.

Verses 13-18:Then Nebuchadnezzar in furious rage commanded that Shadrach, Meshach, and Abednego be brought. Then they brought these men before the king. Nebuchadnezzar said to them, "Is it true, O Shadrach, Meshach, and Abednego, that you do not serve my gods or worship the golden image which I have set up? Now if you are ready when you hear the sound of the horn, pipe, lyre, trigon, harp, bagpipe, and every kind of music, to fall down and worship the image which I have made, well and good; but if you do not worship, you shall immediately be cast into a burning fiery furnace; and who is the god that will deliver you out of my hands?"

Shadrach, Meshach, and Abednego answered the king, "O Nebuchadnezzar, we have no need to answer you in this matter. If it be so, our God whom we serve is able to deliver us from the burning fiery furnace; and he will deliver us out of your hand, O king. But if not, be it known to you, O king, that we will not serve your gods or worship the golden image which you have set up."

Nebuchadnezzar sent for the young men and asked them if the charges were true. He gave them then an opportunity to worship the image with the reminder that no god could deliver them from the flames. A typical martyr story usually emphasizes one of two motifs. Either the persecuted are delivered or they are not, but in neither case do they compromise their basic beliefs and principles. There is something of both motifs in the speech by the three youths. This speech is in reality the climax of the story; the deliverance later is important but anticlimactic. The youths remained steadfast in the face of the danger. They had faith that their God could deliver them from the terror, but they were wise enough to know that he did not always operate in this manner. "If it be [that we are cast into the furnace], our God whom we serve is able to deliver us from the burning fiery furnace; and he will deliver us out of your hand, O king. *But if not,* be it known to you, O king, that we will not serve your gods or worship the golden image which you have set up" (italics added).

Verses 19-30: Then Nebuchadnezzar was full of fury, and the expression of his face was changed against Shadrach, Meshach, and Abednego. He ordered the furnace heated seven times more than it was wont to be heated. And he ordered certain mighty men of his army to bind Shadrach, Meshach, and Abednego, and to cast them into the burning fiery furnace. Then these men were bound in their mantles, their tunics, their hats, and their other garments, and they were cast into the burning fiery furnace. Because the king's order was strict and the furnace very hot, the flame of the fire slew those men who took up Shadrach, Meshach, and Abednego. And these three men, Shadrach, Meshach, and Abednego, fell bound into the burning fiery furnace.

Then King Nebuchadnezzar was astonished and rose up in haste. He said to his counselors, "Did we not cast three men bound into the fire?" They answered the king, "True, O king." He answered, "But I see four men loose, walking in the midst of the fire, and they are not hurt; and the appearance of the fourth is like a son of the gods."

Then Nebuchadnezzar came near to the door of the burning fiery furnace and said, "Shadrach, Meshach, and Abednego, servants of the Most High God, come forth, and come here!" Then Shadrach, Meshach, and Abednego came out from the fire. And the satraps, the prefects, the governors, and the king's counselors gathered together and saw that the fire had not had any power over the bodies of those men; the hair of their heads was not singed, their mantles were not harmed, and no smell of fire had come upon them. Nebuchadnezzar said, "Blessed be the God of Shadrach, Meshach, and Abednego, who has sent his angel and delivered his servants, who trusted in him, and set at nought the king's command, and yielded up their bodies rather than serve and worship any god except their own God. Therefore I make a decree: Any people, nation, or language that speaks anything against the God of Shadrach, Meshach, and Abednego shall be torn limb from limb, and their houses laid in ruins; for there is no other god who is able to deliver in this way." Then the king promoted Shadrach, Meshach, and Abednego in the province of Babylon.

Certainly persons did not speak to the king with such impertinence! The furnace was heated seven times hotter than normal; the heat was so intense that, when the three youths were thrown into the flames, the ones who threw them in were killed by the heat! But something marvelous was occurring. The king saw not three but *four* persons in the fire walking about unhurt! The fourth was like a "son of the gods." This expression in Hebrew idiom meant simply "God."

In other words, the one who was with them was God himself.

The king summoned the three youths to come out of the furnace. An amazing thing had happened. Not even the smell of smoke or fire was on them. Because of their witness, a decree from Nebuchadnezzar was proclaimed to honor the God of Shadrach, Meshach, and Abednego—who, incidentally, were promoted in the service of the king.

Summary

To the people of Judah this story would stir up feelings of mutual appreciation and empathy. They, too, were being required to worship other gods and even in the temple itself there stood an image which they were expected to worship. The courage of the three youths was an inspiration for them not so much because they were delivered from the furnace but because of their defiance in the very face of the king. The forces of this world, arrogant as they were, confident that nothing could stop them and wielding power selfishly rather than for the good of the people, were themselves subject to the God who was over all. The point of the story seems to concentrate not on the deliverance but on the commitment to the one true God in whose service these three, at least, were not afraid to face the ultimate threat.

Questions for Further Consideration

1. What kinds of situations can you think of that are in some ways comparable to the plight of the three youths depicted in this story?

2. Is it always physical martyrdom that threatens to destroy a person? What other types of situations can you envision in which certain actions because of one's religious faith might result in serious consequences? For groups of people? For individuals?

3. How does one deal with such situations?

Chapter 4—Kings Are Also Subject to God

Verses 1-18: King Nebuchadnezzar to all peoples, nations, and languages, that dwell in all the earth: Peace be multiplied to you! It has seemed good to me to show the signs and wonders that the Most High God has wrought toward me.

> How great are his signs,
> how mighty his wonders!
> His kingdom is an everlasting
> kingdom.
> and his dominion is from
> generation to generation.

I, Nebuchadnezzar, was at ease in my house and prospering in my palace. I had a dream which made me afraid; as I lay in bed the fancies and the visions of my head alarmed me. Therefore I made a decree that all the wise men of Babylon should be brought before me, that they might make known to me the interpretation of the dream. Then the magicians, the enchanters, the Chaldeans, and the astrologers came in; and I told them the dream, but they could not make known to me its interpretation. At last Daniel came in before me—he who was named Belteshazzar after the name of my god, and in whom is the spirit of the holy gods—and I told him the dream, saying, "O Belteshazzar, chief of the magicians, because I know that the spirit of the holy gods is in you and that no mystery is difficult for you, here is the dream which I saw; tell me its interpretation. The visions of my head as I lay in bed were these: I saw, and behold, a tree in the midst of the earth; and its height was great. The tree grew and became strong, and its top reached to heaven, and it was visible to the end of the whole earth. Its leaves were fair and its fruit abundant, and in it was food for all. The beasts of the field found shade under it, and the birds of the air dwelt in its branches, and all flesh was fed from it.

"I saw in the visions of my head as I lay in bed, and behold, a watcher, a holy one, came down from heaven. He cried aloud and said thus, 'Hew down the tree and cut off its branches, strip off its leaves and scatter its fruit; let the beasts flee from under it and the birds from its branches. But leave the stump of its roots in the earth, bound with a band of iron and bronze, amid the tender grass of the field. Let him be wet with the dew of heaven; let his lot be with the beasts in the grass of the earth; let his mind be changed from a man's, and let a beast's mind be given to him; and let seven times pass over him. The sentence is by the decree of the watchers, the decision by the word of the holy ones, to the end that the living may know that the Most High rules the kingdom of men, and gives it to whom he will, and sets over it the lowliest of men.' This dream I, King Nebuchadnezzar, saw. And you, O Belteshazzar, declare the interpretation, because all the wise men of my kingdom are not able to make known to me the interpretation, but you are able, for the spirit of the holy gods is in you."

Nebuchadnezzar exalted himself at the beginning of this story. At the height of his greatness he had a dream which the wise men of Babylon could not explain. Daniel, however, finally came to the rescue again to interpret the dream for the king. He had seen a great tree which grew up to heaven, but the tree was cut down and its branches cut off. The stump was to be left in the ground, however, bound with a band of iron and bronze to lie in the fields until "seven times pass over him." (The number seven probably signified a completed period of time.) The king had confidence that Daniel would be able to interpret the dream.

Verses 19-27: Then Daniel, whose name was Belteshazzar, was dismayed for a moment, and his thoughts alarmed him. The king said, "Belteshazzar, let not the dream or the interpretation alarm you." Belteshazzar answered, "My lord, may the dream be for those who hate you and its interpretation for your enemies! The tree you saw, which grew and became strong, so that its top reached to heaven, and it was visible to the end of the whole earth; whose leaves were fair and its fruit abundant, and in which was food for all; under which beasts of the field found shade, and in whose branches the birds of the air dwelt—it is you, O king, who have grown and become strong. Your greatness has grown and reaches to heaven, and your dominion to the ends of the earth. And whereas the king saw a watcher, a holy one, coming down from heaven and saying, 'Hew down the tree and destroy it, but leave the stump of its roots in the earth, bound with a band of iron and bronze, in the tender grass of the field; and let him be wet with the dew of heaven; and let his lot be with the beasts of the field, till seven times pass over him'; this is the interpretation, O king: It is a decree of the Most High, which has come upon my lord the king, that you shall be driven from among men, and your dwelling shall be with the beasts of the field; you shall be made to eat grass like an ox, and you shall be wet with the dew of heaven, and seven times shall pass over you, till you know that the Most High rules the kingdom of men, and gives it to whom he will. And as it was commanded to leave the stump of the roots of the tree, your kingdom shall be sure for you from the time that you know that Heaven rules. Therefore, O king, let my counsel be acceptable to you; break off your sins by practicing righteousness, and your iniquities by showing mercy to the oppressed, that there may perhaps be a lengthening of your tranquillity."

At first Daniel was alarmed about the matter, but the king urged him to proceed. After indicating to the king that he was unhappy with the meaning (verse 19c), Daniel interpreted the dream. The tree represents Nebuchadnezzar, who would suffer from a form of insanity in which a person acts like a wild animal. This is called "insania zoanthropia." He would live as an animal. Daniel urged the king to change his ways by "practicing righteousness" and "showing mercy to the oppressed." It might be that this change could alter the judgment.

Verses 28-33: All this came upon King Nebuchadnezzar. At the end of twelve months he was walking on the roof of the royal palace of Babylon, and the king said, "Is not this great Babylon, which I have built by my mighty power as a royal residence and for the glory of my majesty?" While the words were still in the king's mouth, there fell a voice from heaven, "O King Nebuchadnezzar, to you it is spoken: The kingdom has departed from you, and you shall be driven from among men, and your dwelling shall be with the beasts of the field; and you shall be made to eat grass like an ox; and seven times shall pass over you, until you have learned that the Most High rules the kingdom of men and gives it to whom he will." Immediately the word was fulfilled upon Nebuchadnezzar. He was driven from among men, and ate grass like an ox, and his body was wet with the dew of heaven till his hair grew as long as eagles' feathers, and his nails were like birds' claws.

The king was given a full year, but his arrogance and pride seemed to be undiminished. While he was still boasting, the prediction of Daniel was fulfilled. There may have been a semblance of fact behind this story. Nabonidus, the last king of the Babylonian empire, did spend a period of time at an oasis, at Teima, during some very crucial times in his reign. (The story was transferred in the telling to Nebuchadnezzar who was much better known to the people in Palestine in later times.)

Verses 34-37: At the end of the days I, Nebuchadnezzar, lifted my eyes to heaven, and my reason returned to me, and I blessed the Most High, and praised and honored him who lives for ever;

> for his dominion is an everlasting
> dominion,
> and his kingdom endures from
> generation to generation;
> all the inhabitants of the earth are
> accounted as nothing;
> and he does according to his will
> in the host of heaven
> and among the inhabitants of the
> earth;
> and none can stay his hand
> or say to him, "What doest thou?"

At the same time my reason returned to me; and for the glory of my kingdom, my majesty and splendor returned to me. My counselors and my lords sought me, and I was established in my kingdom, and still more greatness was added to me. Now I, Nebuchadnezzar, praise and extol and honor the King of heaven; for all his works are right and his ways are just; and those who walk in pride he is able to abase.

After the period of the judgment was completed, the king's sanity returned, and at that time he honored the God of heaven and acknowledged that, no matter how great and powerful a human being may become, the God above all is powerful over all!

Summary

This story probably was included in the collection to remind the readers that Antiochus was human and subject to judgment by the God whom they worshiped, Antiochus had called himself Epiphanes (meaning God-manifest), thereby exalting himself in pride and arrogance. The readers and hearers of this story could take heart knowing that his time for an accounting with God was not far off. It is interesting to note that the Jews called him, Epimenes, meaning "madman"!

Questions for Further Consideration

1. What does the delay in the fulfillment of the dream (verses 28-33) say about God's justice and mercy?

2. History is filled with stories about people who had grandiose opinions of themselves. Can you think of any historical figures who exalted themselves only to fall?

3. Can you think of contemporary examples?

4. What were the causes of their fall from the heights as secularly understood? Religiously understood?

Chapter 5—Judgment Surely Comes upon Evil

Verses 1-4: King Belshazzar made a great feast for a thousand of his lords, and drank wine in front of the thousand.

Belshazzar, when he tasted the wine, commanded that the vessels of gold and of silver which Nebuchadnezzar his father had taken out of the temple in Jerusalem be brought, that the king and his lords, his wives, and his concubines might drink from them. Then they brought in the golden and silver vessels which had been taken out of the temple, the house of God in Jerusalem; and the king and his lords, his wives, and his concubines drank from them. They drank wine, and praised the gods of gold and silver, bronze, iron, wood, and stone.

Belshazzar was not technically the king; rather, he ruled in the place of Nabonidus during those periods when the latter was "indisposed" (see discussion of 4:28-33). This feast reflects the atmosphere of idolatry and sacrilege. During such times of revelry pagan deities were toasted; here they were being toasted with the vessels that had been dedicated and were sacred to the God of Israel. This episode may have reminded the Jewish readers and hearers about the sacrilege which Antiochus had committed when he plundered the temple, even stripping gold from its facade.

Verses 5-12: Immediately the fingers of a man's hand appeared and wrote on the plaster of the wall of the king's palace, opposite the lampstand; and the king saw the hand as it wrote. Then the king's color changed, and his thoughts alarmed him; his limbs gave way, and his knees knocked together. The king cried aloud to bring in the enchanters, the Chaldeans, and the astrologers. The king said to the wise men of Babylon, "Whoever reads this writing, and shows me its interpretation, shall be clothed with purple, and have a chain of gold about his neck, and shall be the third ruler in the kingdom." Then all the king's wise men came in, but they could not read the writing or make known to the king the interpretation. Then King Belshazzar was greatly alarmed, and his color changed; and his lords were perplexed.

The queen, because of the words of the king and his lords, came into the banqueting hall; and the queen said, "O king, live for ever! Let not your thoughts alarm you or your color change. There is in your kingdom a man in whom is the spirit of the holy gods. In the days of your father light and understanding and wisdom, like the wisdom of the gods, were found in him, and King Nebuchadnezzar, your father, made him chief of the magicians, enchanters, Chaldeans, and astrologers, because an excellent spirit, knowledge, and understanding to interpret dreams, explain riddles, and solve problems were found in this Daniel, whom the king named Belteshazzar. Now let Daniel be called, and he will show the interpretation."

There appeared in the room the fingers of a man's hand which wrote a message on the wall. Naturally, none of the wise men of Babylon could interpret the message, but the queen (probably the queen-mother) remembered that Daniel was good at such things!

Verses 13-23: Then Daniel was brought in before the king. The king said to Daniel, "You are that Daniel, one of the exiles of Judah, whom the king my father brought from Judah. I have heard of you that the spirit of the holy gods is in you, and that light and understanding and excellent wisdom are found in you. Now the wise men, the enchanters, have been brought in before me to read this writing and make known to me its interpretation; but they could not show the interpretation of the matter. But I have heard that you can give interpretations and solve problems. Now if you can read the writing and make known to me its interpretation, you shall be clothed with purple, and have a chain of gold about your neck, and shall be the third ruler in the kingdom."

Then Daniel answered before the king, "Let your gifts be for yourself, and give your rewards to another; nevertheless, I will read the writing to the king and make known to him the interpretation. O king, the Most High God gave Nebuchadnezzar your father kingship and greatness and glory and majesty; and because of the greatness that he gave him, all peoples, nations, and languages trembled and feared before him; whom he would he slew, and whom he would he kept alive; whom he would he raised up, and whom he would he put down. But when his heart was lifted up and his spirit was hardened so that he dealt proudly, he was deposed from his kingly throne, and his glory was taken from him; he was driven from among men, and his mind was made like that of a beast, and his dwelling was with the wild asses; he was fed grass like an ox, and his body was wet with the dew of heaven, until he knew that the Most High God rules the kingdom of men, and sets over it whom he will. And you his son, Belshazzar, have not humbled your heart, though you knew all this, but you have lifted up yourself against the Lord of heaven; and the vessels of his house have been brought in before you, and you and your lords, your wives, and your concubines have drunk wine from them; and you have praised the gods of silver and gold, of bronze, iron, wood, and stone, which do not see or hear or know, but the God in whose hand is your breath, and whose are all your ways, you have not honored."

Daniel was summoned to the palace, refused the reward offered for the interpretation, and alluded to several of the incidents already recorded in the stories to this point. He described to them why the hand had appeared, that is, because of their sacrilege and idolatry.

Verses 24-31: "Then from his presence the hand was sent, and this writing was inscribed. And this is the writing that was inscribed: MENE, MENE, TEKEL, and PARSIN. This is the interpretation of the matter: MENE, God has numbered the days of your kingdom and brought it to an end; TEKEL, you have been weighed in the balances and found wanting; PERES, your kingdom is divided and given to the Medes and Persians."

Then Belshazzar commanded, and Daniel was clothed with purple, a chain of gold was put about his neck, and proclamation was made concerning him, that he should be the third ruler in the kingdom.

That very night Belshazzar the Chaldean king was slain. And Darius the Mede received the kingdom, being about sixty-two years old.

The writing on the wall was simple Aramaic; the problem lay in interpreting what was written. *Mene* means numbered; *Tekel* means weighed; and *Parsin* means separated or divided. The meaning was that the one true God had *numbered* the days of the kingdom, *weighed* it on the balances of his justice and righteousness and found it lacking; and he had at that point *separated* the kingdom (or divided it) to give it to the Medes and the Persians.

We are told that that very night the kingdom fell to the Medes. It is historically true that Belshazzar was in command when the country fell, but we know of no Darius the Mede. Cyrus overthrew the Babylonian empire. His general was Gobyras who was about sixty-two years old when this occurred. It is possible that he is the one referred to here as "Darius the Mede."

Summary

The simple message of this chapter seems clear enough. Sacrilege and blasphemy against the one true God brought destruction upon the ones who participated in such practices. This chapter also shows some progression in the story which the author was telling. The history predicted in chapter 2 was beginning to run its course. The head of gold (Babylon) had fallen. The author at this point turned to an episode in the life of Daniel during the period of the silver and bronze age depicted in chapter 2.

Questions for Further Consideration

1. What types of modern activities can you think of which are analogous to the "secularized" festivities which took place in this story?

2. What is the appropriate response of a truly "religious" person to such activities?

3. Why are people who behave in this manner "found wanting"?

Chapter 6—God Watches Over the Faithful

Verses 1-5: It pleased Darius to set over the kingdom a hundred and twenty satraps, to be throughout the whole kingdom; and over them three presidents, of whom Daniel was one, to whom these satraps should give account, so that the king might suffer no loss. Then this Daniel became distinguished above all the other presidents and satraps, because an excellent spirit was in him; and the king planned to set him over the whole kingdom. Then the presidents and the satraps sought to find a ground for complaint against Daniel with regard to the kingdom; but they could find no ground for complaint or any fault, because he was faithful, and no error or fault was found in him. Then these men said, "We shall not find any ground for complaint against this Daniel unless we find it in connection with the law of his God."

Even under Median-Persian rule, Daniel, the faithful Israelite, was still trusted and respected by even the king. Organizationally the Persians did establish satraps, i.e., administrative districts, and over these territories certain persons exercised designated powers. Daniel was so good at his job that he was about to be placed in control of the entire kingdom. Human jealousy arose in the other leaders who sought some way to discredit Daniel. Finally they realized that the only way they could do this was through his religious beliefs and practices. Daniel was indeed a man of integrity according to this account.

Verses 6-9: Then these presidents and satraps came by agreement to the king and said to him, "O King Darius, live for ever! All the presidents of the kingdom, the prefects and the satraps, the counselors and the governors are agreed that the king should establish an ordinance and enforce an interdict, that whoever makes petition to any god or man for thirty days, except to you, O king, shall be cast into the den of lions. Now, O king, establish the interdict and sign the document, so that it cannot be changed, according to the law of the Medes and the Persians, which cannot be revoked." Therefore King Darius signed the document and interdict.

The other leaders, appealing to the ego of the king, had a law signed by him forbidding anyone to pray to any god or man except Darius for thirty days. The king signed the law. Anyone who broke this law was to be thrown into a pit filled with lions!

Verses 10-15: When Daniel knew that the document had been signed, he went to his house where he had windows in his upper chamber open toward Jerusalem; and he got down upon his knees three times a day and prayed and gave thanks before his God, as he had done previously. Then these men came by agreement and found Daniel making petition and supplication before his God. Then they came near and said before the king, concerning the interdict, "O king! Did you not sign an interdict, that any man who makes petition to any god or man within thirty days except to you, O king, shall be cast into the den of lions?" The king answered, "The thing stands fast, according to the law of the Medes and Persians, which cannot be revoked." Then they answered before the king, "That Daniel, who is one of the exiles from Judah, pays no heed to you, O king, or the interdict you have signed, but makes his petition three times a day."

Then the king, when he heard these words, was much distressed, and set his mind to deliver Daniel; and he labored till the sun went down to rescue him. Then these men came by agreement to the king, and said to the king, "Know, O king, that it is a law of the Medes and Persians that no interdict or ordinance which the king establishes can be changed."

Daniel, however, continued to pray to his God and was accused before the king of breaking the newly signed law. The king was distressed over the events (and probably felt he had been deceived), but he could find no way around the law's consequences.

Verses 16-24: Then the king commanded, and Daniel was brought and cast into the den of lions. The king said to Daniel, "May your God, whom you serve continually, deliver you!" And a stone was brought and laid upon the mouth of the den, and the king sealed it with his own signet and with the signet of his lords, that nothing might be changed concerning Daniel. Then the king went to his palace, and spent the night fasting; no diversions were brought to him, and sleep fled from him.

Then, at break of day, the king arose and went in haste to the den of lions. When he came near to the den where Daniel was, he cried out in a tone of anguish and said to Daniel, "O Daniel, servant of the living God, has your God, whom you serve continually, been able to deliver you from the lions?" Then Daniel said to the king, "O king, live for ever! My God sent his angel and shut the lions' mouths, and they have not hurt me, because I was found blameless

before him; and also before you, O king, I have done no wrong."
Then the king was exceedingly glad, and commanded that Daniel
be taken up out of the den. So Daniel was taken up out of the den,
and no kind of hurt was found upon him, because he had trusted in
his God. And the king commanded, and those men who had
accused Daniel were brought and cast into the den of lions—they,
their children, and their wives; and before they reached the bottom
of the den the lions overpowered them and broke all their bones in
pieces.

Daniel was then brought and thrown into the pit which was
covered with a stone and sealed with the king's signet. Darius hoped
that Daniel's God would be able to deliver him, but his hopes were
slight. The king's distress was clearly shown because "no diversions"
were brought to him during the night! At dawn the king went to see
what remained of poor Daniel. To his great amazement, Daniel was
alive! Both those who had plotted against Daniel and their families
were thrown into the pit and were attacked "before they reached the
bottom" of the pit.

Verses 25-28: Then King Darius wrote to all the peoples, nations,
and languages that dwell in all the earth: "Peace be multiplied to
you. I make a decree, that in all my royal dominion men tremble
and fear before the God of Daniel,

for he is the living God,
    enduring for ever;
his kingdom shall never be destroyed,
    and his dominion shall be to the
        end.
He delivers and rescues,
    he works signs and wonders
    in heaven and on earth,
he who has saved Daniel
    from the power of the lions."
So this Daniel prospered during the reign of Darius and the reign
of Cyrus the Persian.

Again the God whom Daniel served was exalted in the kingdom,
and Daniel continued to serve in this situation.

Summary
This story is quite similar in many ways to that found in chapter 3.

It is basically a martyr story, but a new motif has been added: the idea of the trial by ordeal. Daniel survived because his God was with him and he was innocent; his enemies suffered the same fate they had plotted for Daniel. Note in this the element of poetic justice.

In summarizing the first six chapters we could say that there emerges a definite historical progression in the arrangement of the stories. It is obvious also that the author was attempting to illustrate those points which would be most familiar to those who would read and hear these stories. The decrees forbidding the Jewish people to worship their God or to practice their religious obligations, the striking down of those who exalted themselves above the God of Israel—all these matters would strike responsive chords in the minds and hearts of those who heard or read these words.

There is another aspect to these stories which most commentators overlook. It is that Daniel and his friends served in the courts of foreign and pagan kings, accepting by necessity some of the cultural trappings of their captors. And it is interesting to note that these activities on the part of Daniel and his friends were not condemned but rather highlighted in such a way as to encourage openness on the part of those who read and heard.

It is also possible that one of the purposes of the writer was to demonstrate to the political authorities, if indeed they were reading the book, that the Jewish people could and would be valuable assets to the administrative structure of the government if given the opportunity. All they asked in return was the freedom to worship as they felt they must. And none of their religious customs or practices was subversive!

Questions for Further Consideration

1. In what ways do people today attempt to use the religious commitments of others to "entrap" them?

2. Under what kinds of circumstances is it legitimate to "go against the law"?

3. What kind of response should a truly religious person in a position of authority have when faced with the enforcement of "bad laws"?

4. If a religious person truly believes a law cannot be obeyed because of religious obligations, what kind of response should that person expect from the governmental authorities? Why?

Chapter 7—The Vision of the Beasts and the Son of Man

The last six chapters of the book of Daniel are different from the first six, which were delightful stories about Jewish youths in a foreign land fighting to fulfill their religious obligations. But with chapter 7 the literary genre changes to that known as apocalyptic, and to these chapters we now turn.

Verses 1-8: In the first year of Belshazzar king of Babylon, Daniel had a dream and visions of his head as he lay in his bed. Then he wrote down the dream, and told the sum of the matter. Daniel said, "I saw in my vision by night, and behold, the four winds of heaven were stirring up the great sea. And four great beasts came up out of the sea, different from one another. The first was like a lion and had eagles' wings. Then as I looked its wings were plucked off, and it was lifted up from the ground and made to stand upon two feet like a man; and the mind of a man was given to it. And behold, another beast, a second one, like a bear. It was raised up on one side; it had three ribs in its mouth between its teeth; and it was told, 'Arise, devour much flesh.' After this I looked, and lo, another, like a leopard, with four wings of a bird on its back; and the beast had four heads; and dominion was given to it. After this I saw in the night visions, and behold, a fourth beast, terrible and dreadful and exceedingly strong; and it had great iron teeth; it devoured and broke in pieces, and stamped the residue with its feet. It was different from all the beasts that were before it; and it had ten horns. I considered the horns, and behold, there came up among them another horn, a little one, before which three of the first horns were plucked up by the roots; and behold, in this horn were eyes like the eyes of a man, and a mouth speaking great things."

Here we find the traditional apocalyptic usage of the vision. It is interesting that we are told that Daniel wrote down the dream, the "sum of the matter." The sea in apocalyptic literature usually symbolizes the source from which evil or the agents of evil emerge. The background for this is found in the mythologies of the ancient world, some of which are reflected in the Old Testament.

The four beasts represent four world empires (compare with the image of Nebuchadnezzar in chapter 2). The first, "like a lion with eagles' wings," is Babylon. The second, "like a bear," is Media, noted for its greed and often savage activities. The third, "like a leopard" (or panther), represents Persia, and the *four* wings and *four* heads probably symbolize its "world-wide" dominion. The last beast with great iron teeth (compare with the iron legs of the image in chapter 2) is the Greek empire and its successors. The ten horns represent the total or completed number of kings among which emerged the "little horn" (Antiochus) who came to power by overcoming three other claimants to the throne. This horn had eyes and a mouth "speaking great things."

Verses 9-10:
"As I looked,
thrones were placed
  and one that was ancient of days
    took his seat;
his raiment was white as snow,
  and the hair of his head like pure wool;
his throne was fiery flames,
  its wheels were burning fire.
A stream of fire issued
  and came forth from before him;
a thousand thousands served him,
  and ten thousand times ten
    thousand stood before him;
the court sat in judgment,
  and the books were opened."

It is interesting that in this chapter the sections dealing with the deity are in poetic form and those dealing with Daniel's visions and thoughts are in prose. The scene shifts to a throne set for judgment. (The scene itself is called a "theophany." This means an "appearance of God," and this type of scene is found throughout the pages of the Old and New Testaments. It usually appears in crisis situations where God is present at a particular time in a particular place to accomplish a particular purpose.)

The figure was clothed in white, a symbol of victory and power, with a head of hair, depicting wisdom, justice, and integrity. The numbers of those who served were multiples of ten, the number symbolizing completeness. The scene took place in a court, and the books were opened.

Verses 11-12: "I looked then because of the sound of the great words which the horn was speaking. And as I looked, the beast was slain, and its body destroyed and given over to be burned with fire. As for the rest of the beasts, their dominion was taken away, but their lives were prolonged for a season and a time."

The last beast was slain and was to be destroyed with fire, but the other three beasts were *not* destroyed. Their power was taken away, but they were allowed to continue in existence for a while longer.

Verses 13-14:
"I saw in the night visions,
and behold, with the clouds of
          heaven
     there came one like a son of man,
and he came to the Ancient of Days
     and was presented before him.
And to him was given dominion
     and glory and kingdom,
that all peoples, nations, and
     languages
          should serve him;
     his dominion is an everlasting
          dominion,
     which shall not pass away,
and his kingdom one
          that shall not be destroyed."

Then, in a further development of the scene, Daniel saw one like a "son of man" (the Hebrew idiom for "man"). This person came in the clouds—whether by ascending or descending is not clear. It is obvious, too, that the author wished to draw a dramatic contrast between this person and the beastly kingdoms already described. To this person was given power and authority to rule in a kingdom which would not be extinguished. It may be that the term "son of man" should be translated and interpreted here as "beloved man" (see verses 21-22). The usage would then be analogous to the term used so often in the Old Testament, "Daughter of Zion," which means "beloved Zion."

Verses 15-22: "As for me, Daniel, my spirit within me was anxious and the visions of my head alarmed me. I approached one of those who stood there and asked him the truth concerning all this. So he told me, and made known to me the interpretation of the things. 'These four great beasts are four kings who shall arise out of the earth. But the saints of the Most High shall receive the kingdom, and possess the kingdom for ever, for ever and ever.'
"Then I desired to know the truth concerning the fourth beast,

which was different from all the rest, exceedingly terrible, with its teeth of iron and claws of bronze; and which devoured and broke in pieces, and stamped the residue with its feet; and concerning the ten horns that were on its head, and the other horn which came up and before which three of them fell, the horn which had eyes and a mouth that spoke great things, and which seemed greater than its fellows. As I looked, this horn made war with the saints, and prevailed over them, until the Ancient of Days came, and judgment was given for the saints of the Most High, and the time came when the saints received the kingdom.

Daniel then, as most apocalyptic "seers," was puzzled over what he had seen. He asked one of those standing around (probably an angel) about the meaning of all this. The four beasts were four kingdoms, but the son of man, or "beloved man," represented the "saints of the Most High." These saints were understood as those faithful to the God of Israel. It was to them that the final and decisive rule was given; the kingdom given to them was of such a kind that it would never be destroyed. It was God's kingdom of which they were custodians.

The interpreter then answered Daniel's inquiry concerning the fourth beast which was so different. He explained (verse 21) that this little horn had made war on the saints.

> Verses 23-28:
> "Thus he said: 'As for the fourth
>   beast,
> there shall be a fourth kingdom on
>   earth,
>   which shall be different from all
>   the kingdoms,
> and it shall devour the whole earth,
>   and trample it down, and break
>   it to pieces.
> As for the ten horns,
> out of this kingdom
>   ten kings shall arise,
>   and another shall arise after them;
> he shall be different from the former
>   ones,
>   and shall put down three kings.
> He shall speak words against the
>   Most High,

and shall wear out the saints of the
Most High,
and shall think to change the
times and the law;
and they shall be given into his hand
for a time, two times, and half a
time.
But the court shall sit in judgment,
and his dominion shall be taken
away,
to be consumed and destroyed to
the end.
And the kingdom and the
dominion
and the greatness of the kingdoms
under the whole heaven
shall be given to the people of
the saints of the Most High;
their kingdom shall be an
everlasting kingdom,
and all dominions shall serve and
obey them.'

"Here is the end of the matter. As for me, Daniel, my thoughts greatly alarmed me, and my color changed; but I kept the matter in my mind."

The angel explained what Daniel had seen, especially with regard to the little horn. It is clear from verse 25 that the writer assumed that the identity of this king would be known from the description. He would blaspheme, persecute the people of God, and proscribe their religion; they would be under this persecution for a completed but brief period of time (i.e., three and one-half years). He would be judged by God and would receive his deserved penalty. The real dominion or power in this world would then be delegated to the saints of the Most High. These saints would exercise his sovereignty in the world.

The seer—in this case, Daniel—was alarmed and puzzled. From his historical perspective, he could not understand the riddle which had just been explained. But those who were reading or hearing the vision would know what to make of these scenes. They would know that they were living in the times about which Daniel purportedly had written.

Summary

In this chapter we find the connecting link between chapters 1-6 and chapters 7-12, for chapter 7 is almost an exact replica of chapter 2 in terms of the succession of world empires. The events of chapter 7, however, go much further in identifying the more specific problems of the Maccabean era. The reader, in comparing the two chapters, can see how apocalyptic imagery is used in chapter 7 and also how it is usually interpreted for the reader if one reads far enough! One of the often missed religious points is the teaching that some evil can be punished and left to survive. Some evil, however, *must* be completely destroyed!

Questions for Further Consideration

1. What do you think of the idea that God's people are to rule the earth? What kind of responsibility does this place upon those who claim to be the people of God?

2. Reread the chapter carefully and interpret the numbers in accordance with the symbolic meanings given in chapter 1 of this book.

3. In the light of the teaching that some evil is allowed to remain and some evil is destroyed, what do you think the author had in mind about God's judgment? Is the "end of the world" really being discussed here? If so , where? What kind of teaching about judgment is being espoused? Can you think of contemporary examples which illustrate these aspects of judgment?

Chapter 8—The Apocalyptic Survey of the History of the Period

Verses 1-14: In the third year of the reign of King Belshazzar a vision appeared to me, Daniel, after that which appeared to me at the first. And I saw in the vision; and when I saw, I was in Susa the capital, which is in the province of Elam; and I saw in the vision, and I was at the river Ulai. I raised my eyes and saw, and behold, a ram standing on the bank of the river. It had two horns; and both horns were high, but one was higher than the other, and the higher one came up last. I saw the ram charging westward and northward and southward; no beast could stand before him, and there was no one who could rescue from his power; he did as he pleased and magnified himself. As I was considering, behold, a he-goat came from the west across the face of the whole earth, without touching the ground; and the goat had a conspicuous horn between his eyes. He came to the ram with the two horns, which I had seen standing on the bank of the river, and he ran at him in his mighty wrath. I saw him come close to the ram, and he was enraged against him and struck the ram and broke his two horns; and the ram had no power to stand before him, but he cast him down to the ground and trampled upon him; and there was no one who could rescue the ram from his power. Then the he-goat magnified himself exceedingly; but when he was strong, the great horn was broken, and instead of it there came up four conspicuous horns toward the four winds of heaven.

Out of one of them came forth a little horn, which grew exceedingly great toward the south, toward the east, and toward the glorious land. It grew great, even to the host of heaven; and some of the host of the stars it cast down to the ground, and trampled upon them. It magnified itself, even up to the Prince of the host; and the continual burnt offering was taken away from him, and the place of his sanctuary was overthrown. And the host was given over to it together with the continual burnt offering through transgression; and truth was cast down to the ground, and the horn acted and prospered. Then I heard a holy one speaking; and another holy one said to the one that spoke, "For how long is the vision concerning the continual burnt offering, the transgression that makes desolate, and the giving over of the sanctuary and host to be trampled under foot?" And he said to him, "For two thousand and three hundred evenings and mornings; then the sanctuary shall be restored to its rightful state."

Daniel had a second vision. In it he saw a ram with two horns standing on the bank of a river. The location of this river was the same as that of one of the capitals of the Median-Persian Empire. The two horns represented two kingdoms: the first and smaller was Media; the second and larger was Persia. At its zenith the Persian Empire was one of the greatest of the ancient world.

At this point (verse 5) there came from the west a large he-goat, moving so rapidly that he appeared not even to touch the ground. The large horn between his eyes represented Alexander the Great, and the he-goat himself represented the Greek invasion of the area in 334–331 B.C. The he-goat then defeated the ram and exalted himself. At that point the great horn was broken, i.e., Alexander died. We know about Alexander's dream of world conquest and rule; he even entertained notions of a common religion to assist in holding together the large disparate groups. He would place himself at the head of this religion. It is easy to understand that the writer of Daniel felt that this was perhaps the judgment of God on such human self-exaltation. In place of the broken large horn there appeared four smaller horns. These represented the four kingdoms which were finally established after the wars among Alexander's generals.

Another "little horn" emerged from one of the four (verse 9). The description, given in symbolic form in verses 10-12, made it clear that Antiochus was indeed this "little horn" and illustrated much of what we know about the policies of Antiochus toward Judaism at the time he issued his proscription of the Jewish religion. An angel asked how long this would be allowed to continue. The answer is 2,300 evenings and mornings, or approximately three and one-half years! Then the sanctuary of God would return to its rightful state (verse 14). There is some difference of opinion as to whether the figure given here is a figure to be taken symbolically or one to be taken literally; we know that the actual time between the desecration of the temple and its restoration was three years. It is probably better, since the writer was obviously writing *before* that event had occurred, to interpret this as the usual apocalyptic number three and one-half which symbolizes the short period in which evil was allowed to work its cruelty with the conviction that evil would soon be destroyed. At the end of that period the temple (and all that it symbolized) would be "restored to its rightful place." We do not find, incidentally, any thought of an end to history or even the establishment of a supra-historical era. Rather we find a conviction that those who persecute God's elect would come under judgment, and proper worship of God could resume.

Verses 15-17: When I, Daniel, had seen the vision, I sought to understand it; and behold, there stood before me one having the appearance of a man. And I heard a man's voice between the banks of the Ulai, and it called, "Gabriel, make this man understand the vision." So he came near where I stood; and when he came, I was frightened and fell upon my face. But he said to me, "Understand, O son of man, that the vision is for the time of the end."

Verses 15-17 describe a typical apocalyptic scene. The one who saw the vision was puzzled and confused by it; therefore, an interpreter (usually an angel) explained the meaning. In this instance Gabriel told Daniel the meaning but made it clear to him that the events he related were for "the time of the end." (Note: this was not the "end of time"!)

Verses 18-27: As he was speaking to me, I fell into a deep sleep with my face to the ground; but he touched me and set me on my feet. He said, "Behold, I will make known to you what shall be at the latter end of the indignation; for it pertains to the appointed time of the end. As for the ram which you saw with the two horns, these are the kings of Media and Persia. And the he-goat is the king of Greece; and the great horn between his eyes is the first king. As for the horn that was broken, in place of which four others arose, four kingdoms shall arise from his nation, but not with his power. And at the latter end of their rule, when the transgressors have reached their full measure, a king of bold countenance, one who understands riddles, shall arise. His power shall be great, and he shall cause fearful destruction, and shall succeed in what he does, and destroy mighty men and the people of the saints. By his cunning he shall make deceit prosper under his hand, and in his own mind he shall magnify himself. Without warning he shall destroy many; and he shall even rise up against the Prince of princes; but, by no human hand, he shall be broken. The vision of the evenings and the mornings which has been told is true; but seal up the vision, for it pertains to many days hence."
And I, Daniel, was overcome and lay sick for some days; then I rose and went about the king's business; but I was appalled by the vision and did not understand it.

The interpretation is then given. The ram represents Media and Persia, the he-goat the kingdom of Greece, and the great horn the first king! Four nations will arise from the one empire; after a period of time another king will arise who will destroy the people of God and exalt himself. He will challenge God, but God will destroy him. The vision was for "many days hence," and Daniel himself did not understand it. But the people of the Maccabean era did!

Summary

The chapter really explains itself. It is perhaps enough at this point to say that it is typical of apocalyptic writing and methodology.

Questions for Further Consideration

1. How does understanding the history of the period immediately prior to the time of the persecution depicted in the apocalyptic writing aid in interpreting apocalyptic literature?

2. To what does the term "time of the end" refer?

3. Why do you think so many have thought of this as the "end of the world"?

Chapter 9—The Apocalyptic History, cont.

Verses 1-2: In the first year of Darius the son of Ahasu-erus, by birth a Mede, who became king over the realm of the Chaldeans—in the first year of his reign, I, Daniel, perceived in the books the number of years which, according to the word of the LORD to Jeremiah the prophet, must pass before the end of the desolations of Jerusalem, namely, seventy years.

The "meaning" of a prophecy in the book of Jeremiah was revealed to Daniel. It was Jeremiah's conviction that the people of Judah would remain in exile for seventy years (see Jeremiah 25:11-12; 29:10), after which time God would restore them in their land. Whether Jeremiah meant to use the number 70 with a literal meaning or whether he meant it to signify simply a long completed period of time is uncertain. The people did not, however, remain in captivity for seventy years! That this point disturbed some persons is reflected in Zechariah (1:12) and Second Chronicles (36:21). The author of the book of Daniel came up with an ingenious scheme which, he believed, would solve the problem and speak to his existential situation.

Verses 3-19: Then I turned my face to the Lord God, seeking him by prayer and supplications with fasting and sackcloth and ashes. I prayed to the LORD my God and made confession, saying, "O Lord, the great and terrible God, who keepest covenant and steadfast love with those who love him and keep his commandments, we have sinned and done wrong and acted wickedly and rebelled, turning aside from thy commandments and ordinances; we have not listened to thy servants the prophets, who spoke in thy name to our kings, our princes, and our fathers, and to all the people of the land. To thee, O Lord, belongs righteousness, but to us confusion of face, as at this day, to the men of Judah, to the inhabitants of Jerusalem, and to all Israel, those that are near and those that are far away, in all the lands to which thou hast driven them, because of the treachery which they have committed against thee. To us, O Lord, belongs confusion of face, to our kings, to our princes, and to our fathers, because we have sinned against thee. To the Lord our God belong mercy and forgiveness; because we have rebelled against him, and have not obeyed the voice of the Lord our God by following his laws, which he set before us by his servants the prophets. All Israel has trangressed thy law and turned aside, refusing to obey thy voice. And the curse and oath which are written in the law of Moses the servant of God have been poured out upon us, because we have sinned against him. He has confirmed his words, which he spoke against us and against our rulers who ruled us, by bringing upon us a great calamity; for under the whole heaven there has not been done the like of what has been done against Jerusalem. As it is written in the law of Moses, all this calamity has come upon us, yet we have not entreated the favor of the LORD our God, turning from our iniquities and giving heed to thy truth. Therefore the LORD has kept ready the calamity and has brought it upon us; for the LORD our God is righteous in all the works which he has done, and we have not obeyed his voice. And now, O Lord our God, who didst bring thy people out of the land of Egypt with a mighty hand, and hast made thee a name, as at this day, we have sinned, we have done wickedly. O Lord, according to all thy righteous acts, let thy anger and thy wrath turn away from thy city Jerusalem, thy holy hill; because for our sins, and for the iniquities of our fathers, Jerusalem and thy people have become a byword among all who are round about us. Now therefore, O our God, hearken to the prayer of thy servant and to his supplications, and for thy own sake, O Lord, cause thy face to shine upon thy sanctuary, which is desolate. O my God, incline thy ear and hear; open thy eyes and behold our desolations, and the city which is called by thy name; for we do not present our supplications before thee on the ground of our righteousness, but on the ground of thy great mercy. O LORD, hear; O LORD, forgive; O LORD, give heed and act; delay not for thy own sake, O my God, because thy city and thy people are called by thy name."

Before the interpretation was revealed to Daniel, however, he engaged in a long prayer of confession. He acknowledged his own sin and that of the people. Whether this was a general confession, a confession about those who had become apostate, or a confession whose purpose it was to rally the people to keep the faith is not precisely known. It is interesting to note in verse 17 the reference to "your sanctuary, which is desolate," which points to the desecration of the temple by Antiochus.

Verses 20-23: While I was speaking and praying, confessing my sin and the sin of my people Israel, and presenting my supplication before the LORD my God for the holy hill of my God; while I was speaking in prayer, the man Gabriel, whom I had seen in the vision at the first, came to me in swift flight at the time of the evening sacrifice. He came and he said to me, "O Daniel, I have now come out to give you wisdom and understanding. At the beginning of your supplications a word went forth, and I have come to tell it to you, for you are greatly beloved; therefore consider the word and understand the vision."

Daniel had confessed his sin and made a special plea for the "holy hill of my God." Then at the time of the evening sacrifice, Gabriel, Daniel's interpreter, came to explain the message of Jeremiah.

Verses 24-27: "Seventy weeks of years are decreed concerning your people and your holy city, to finish the transgression, to put an end to sin, and to atone for iniquity, to bring in everlasting righteousness, to seal both vision and prophet, and to anoint a most holy place. Know therefore and understand that from the going forth of the word to restore and build Jerusalem to the coming of an anointed one, a prince, there shall be seven weeks. Then for sixty-two weeks it shall be built again with squares and moat, but in a troubled time. And after the sixty-two weeks, an anointed one shall be cut off, and shall have nothing; and the people of the prince who is to come shall destroy the city and the sanctuary. Its end shall come with a flood, and to the end there shall be war; desolations are decreed. And he shall make a strong covenant with many for one week; and for half of the week he shall cause sacrifice and offering to cease; and upon the wing of abominations shall come one who makes desolate, until the decreed end is poured out on the desolator."

It was made clear that the suffering had come upon the people because of sin. Even the sins of the people of God had to be punished (a familiar biblical as well as apocalyptic theme)! According to the author of Daniel the 70 years Jeremiah predicted were really 70 *weeks* of years (490 years) which were divided into 7, 62, and 1 week years. Exactly where the "going forth of the word" was to be dated is unclear; but it does seem clear that the anointed prince was Cyrus (see Isaiah 45:1ff.); therefore, the beginning would be 539 B.C. If the figures are then to be taken as generally correct (they were probably never meant to be taken literally, only to illustrate the point!), the periods would be 587–539; 539–170; 170–164. The reference in verse 26 to an anointed one "cut off" is in all probability to Onias III, the legitimate high priest who was murdered in 170 B.C. There then would come one who would cause "sacrifice and offering to cease" for half a week (3½ again!). It is assumed that the 3½ came at the end of that last week at which time the end would be decreed for the "desolator."

It should be noted that the middle period, 539–170, is not 434 years (62 x 7), but that should not worry a reader of apocalyptic literature. Most numbers given in apocalyptic writings are symbolic, and the 490 years is simply an ingenious device the author has utilized indicating a long completed period of time. He used Jeremiah's figure of the 70 years as a basis, but his real point seems to be that not only the period of the exile was a punishment for Judah's sins but the periods following as well, continuing to the present time. Evil aligned against God and his people would be crushed and the people of God would enjoy a period of peace, prosperity, and power which they had not experienced in many years.

Chapters 10–11—The Apocalyptic History, cont.

Verses 1-9: In the third year of Cyrus king of Persia a word was revealed to Daniel, who was named Belteshazzar. And the word was true, and it was a great conflict. And he understood the word and had understanding of the vision. In those days I, Daniel, was mourning for three weeks. I ate no delicacies, no meat or wine entered my mouth, nor did I anoint myself at all, for the full three weeks. On the twenty-fourth day of the first month, as I was standing on the bank of the great river, that is, the Tigris, I lifted up my eyes and looked, and behold, a man clothed in linen, whose loins were girded with gold of Uphaz. His body was like beryl, his face like the appearance of lightning, his eyes like flaming torches, his arms and legs like the gleam of burnished bronze, and the sound of his words like the noise of a multitude. And I, Daniel, alone saw the vision, for the men who were with me did not see the vision, but a great trembling fell upon them, and they fled to hide themselves. So I was left alone and saw this great vision, and no strength was left in me; my radiant appearance was fearfully changed, and I retained no strength. Then I heard the sound of his words; and when I heard the sound of his words, I fell on my face in a deep sleep with my face to the ground.

Daniel received another revelation. He had been fasting for three weeks and saw a vision which overwhelmed him.

Verses 10-14: And behold, a hand touched me and set me trembling on my hands and knees. And he said to me, "O Daniel, man greatly beloved, give heed to the words that I speak to you, and stand upright, for now I have been sent to you." While he was speaking this word to me, I stood up trembling. Then he said to me, "Fear not, Daniel, for from the first day that you set your mind to understand and humbled yourself before your God, your words have been heard, and I have come because of your words. The prince of the kingdom of Persia withstood me twenty-one days; but Michael, one of the chief princes, came to help me, so I left him there with the prince of the kingdom of Persia and came to make you understand what is to befall your people in the latter days. For the vision is for days yet to come."

It was explained to Daniel that he was to see what would happen to his people in the "latter" days. The angels were delayed because the forces of evil did not want the revelation to be made to Daniel. By this period of history a rather complex angelology and demonology were developing, part of which taught that each nation had a patron spirit. Michael was thought to be the patron angel of the Jews.

10:15–11:1: When he had spoken to me according to these words, I turned my face toward the ground and was dumb. And behold, one in the likeness of the sons of men touched my lips; then I opened my mouth and spoke. I said to him who stood before me, "O my lord, by reason of the vision pains have come upon me, and I retain no strength. How can my lord's servant talk with my lord? For now no strength remains in me, and no breath is left in me."

Again one having the appearance of a man touched me and strengthened me. And he said, "O man greatly beloved, fear not, peace be with you; be strong and of good courage." And when he spoke to me, I was strengthened and said, "Let my lord speak, for you have strengthened me." Then he said, "Do you know why I have come to you? But now I will return to fight against the prince of Persia; and when I am through with him, lo, the prince of Greece will come. But I will tell you what is inscribed in the book of truth: there is none who contends by my side against these except Michael, your prince. And as for me, in the first year of Darius the Mede, I stood up to confirm and strengthen him."

Daniel had a discussion with the angel about his (Daniel's) worthiness to receive the revelation. The "book of truth" supposedly contained an historical account of the period up to the time of the writer (i.e., approximately 165 B.C.).

Verses 2-4: "And now I will show you the truth. Behold, three more kings shall arise in Persia; and a fourth shall be far richer than all of them; and when he has become strong through his riches, he shall stir up all against the kingdom of Greece. Then a mighty king shall arise, who shall rule with great dominion and do according to his will. And when he has arisen, his kingdom shall be broken and divided toward the four winds of heaven, but not to his posterity, not according to the dominion with which he ruled; for his kingdom shall be plucked up and go to others besides these."

The history of Persia and of Alexander was given in a brief statement. The stage was set for a detailed look at more current events after the death of the "mighty king" (Alexander the Great) and the activities of the four lesser kingdoms.

Verses 5-9: "Then the king of the south shall be strong, but one of his princes shall be stronger than he and his dominion shall be a great dominion. After some years they shall make an alliance, and the daughter of the king of the south shall come to the king of the north to make peace; but she shall not retain the strength of her arm, and he and his offspring shall not endure; but she shall be given up, and her attendants, her child, and he who got possession of her.

"In those times a branch from her roots shall arise in his place; he shall come against the army and enter the fortress of the king of the north, and he shall deal with them and shall prevail. He shall also carry off to Egypt their gods with their molten images and with their precious vessels of silver and of gold; and for some years he shall refrain from attacking the king of the north. Then the latter shall come into the realm of the king of the south but shall return into his own land."

The "king of the south" represents Ptolemy I of Egypt, and the "one greater" belonged to the "north," namely the Seleucid line; scholars identify him as Seleucus I. The episode of verse 6 occurred in approximately 250 B.C. when Ptolemy II and Antiochus II made an alliance in which Ptolemy's daughter, Berenice, was to be married to Antiochus. But these persons were all killed, quite possibly by Antiochus's former wife, Laodice.

In verse 7 we read of a "branch," who can be identified as Ptolemy III, who made an invasion and conquered a large area—presumably to avenge the death of his sister. Upon his return to Egypt he was content to remain there, and during that time Seleucus II recaptured part of the conquered territory.

Verses 10-20: "His sons shall wage war and assemble a multitude of great forces, which shall come on and overflow and pass through, and again shall carry the war as far as his fortress. Then the king of the south, moved with anger, shall come out and fight with the king of the north; and he shall raise a great multitude, but it shall be given into his hand. And when the multitude is taken, his heart shall be exalted, and he shall cast down tens of thousands, but he shall not prevail. For the king of the north shall again raise a multitude, greater than the former; and after some years he shall come on with a great army and abundant supplies.

"In those times many shall rise against the king of the south; and the men of violence among your own people shall lift themselves up in order to fulfil the vision; but they shall fail. Then the king of the north shall come and throw up siegeworks, and take a well-fortified city. And the forces of the south shall not stand, or even his picked troops, for there shall be no strength to stand. But he who comes against him shall do according to his own will, and none shall stand before him; and he shall stand in the glorious land, and all of it shall be in his power. He shall set his face to come with the strength of his whole kingdom, and he shall bring terms of peace and perform them. He shall give him the daughter of women to destroy the kingdom; but it shall not stand or be to his advantage. Afterward he shall turn his face to the coastlands, and shall take many of them; but a commander shall put an end to his insolence; indeed he shall turn his insolence back upon him. Then he shall turn his face back toward the fortresses of his own land; but he shall stumble and fall, and shall not be found.

"Then shall arise in his place one who shall send an exactor of tribute through the glory of the kingdom; but within a few days he shall be broken, neither in anger nor in battle."

The "sons" probably refer to Seleucus III and Antiochus III who continued to fight against Egypt. The cryptic references in these verses can be deciphered by looking at almost any good historical account of this period.

Verses 21-28: "In his place shall arise a contemptible person to whom royal majesty has not been given; he shall come in without warning and obtain the kingdom by flatteries. Armies shall be utterly swept away before him and broken, and the prince of the covenant also. And from the time that an alliance is made with him he shall act deceitfully; and he shall become strong with a small people. Without warning he shall come into the richest parts of the province; and he shall do what neither his fathers nor his fathers' fathers have done, scattering among them plunder, spoil, and goods. He shall devise plans against strongholds, but only for a time. And he shall stir up his power and his courage against the king of the south with a great army; and the king of the south shall wage war with an exceedingly great and mighty army; but he shall not stand, for plots shall be devised against him. Even those who eat his rich food shall be his undoing; his army shall be swept away, and many shall fall down slain. And as for the two kings, their minds shall be bent on mischief; they shall speak lies at the same table, but to no avail; for the end is yet to be at the time appointed.

And he shall return to his land with great substance, but his heart shall be set against the holy covenant. And he shall work his will, and return to his own land."

Beginning with verse 21 the author described Antiochus IV. The "prince of the covenant" in verse 22 is probably a reference to Onias III and verses 24 and following tell of Antiochus's temple desecration when he took the gold vessels and stripped away the gold facade.

Verses 29-39: "At the time appointed he shall return and come into the south; but it shall not be this time as it was before. For ships of Kittim shall come against him, and he shall be afraid and withdraw, and shall turn back and be enraged and take action against the holy covenant. He shall turn back and give heed to those who forsake the holy covenant. Forces from him shall appear and profane the temple and fortress, and shall take away the continual burnt offering. And they shall set up the abomination that makes desolate. He shall seduce with flattery those who violate the covenant; but the people who know their God shall stand firm and take action. And those among the people who are wise shall make many understand, though they shall fall by sword and flame, by captivity and plunder, for some days. When they fall, they shall receive a little help. And many shall join themselves to them with flattery; and some of those who are wise shall fall, to refine and to cleanse them and to make them white, until the time of the end, for it is yet for the time appointed.

"And the king shall do according to his will; he shall exalt himself and magnify himself above every god, and shall speak astonishing things against the God of gods. He shall prosper till the indignation is accomplished; for what is determined shall be done. He shall give no heed to the gods of his fathers, or to the one beloved by women; he shall not give heed to any other god, for he shall magnify himself above all. He shall honor the god of fortresses instead of these; a god whom his fathers did not know he shall honor with gold and silver, with precious stones and costly gifts. He shall deal with the strongest fortresses by the help of a foreign god; those who acknowledge him he shall magnify with honor. He shall make them rulers over many and shall divide the land for a price."

These verses explain the situation when Antiochus proscribed Judaism and set up the statue of Zeus in the temple (this is the infamous "abomination of desolation"). The author made it clear that there were many who were in agreement with these actions and who would be apostate, but he urged the readers to remain loyal to their God.

> Verses 40-45: "At the time of the end the king of the south shall attack him; but the king of the north shall rush upon him like a whirlwind, with chariots and horsemen, and with many ships; and he shall come into countries and shall overflow and pass through. He shall come into the glorious land. And tens of thousands shall fall, but these shall be delivered out of his hand: Edom and Moab and the main part of the Ammonites. He shall stretch out his hand against the countries, and the land of Egypt shall not escape. He shall become ruler of the treasures of gold and of silver, and all the precious things of Egypt; and the Libyans and the Ethiopians shall follow in his train. But tidings from the east and the north shall alarm him, and he shall go forth with great fury to exterminate and utterly destroy many. And he shall pitch his palatial tents between the sea and the glorious holy mountain; yet he shall come to his end, with none to help him."

With verse 40 the author ceased to describe what he knew had happened historically and began to predict what would happen. It was his contention that the "king of the south" (the Egyptian ruler) would attack and that Antiochus would die somewhere in Palestine between the sea and the "glorious holy mountain." The typical apocalyptic motif of a great and terrible time immediately before the time of God's intervention (usually accompanied and/or caused by wars and intense suffering, verses 41-43) is present here.

Summary

These chapters are quite in keeping with the usual apocalyptic device, that of recounting history as a prophecy. This was done, in part, to bolster the spirits of those undergoing persecution. For if the evil "foreseen" by Daniel had in fact occurred as predicted, would not the end of the evil tyrant come to pass as well? This "review of history" primarily reaffirmed the author's own conviction and sincere belief that history was not haphazardly drifting here and there, but that it had a purpose, the purpose of the great and true God who could and would set that course anew when the tyrannical forces of evil threatened to destroy all that belonged to Him. It was God, not Antiochus, who was in control. Antiochus did not die in Palestine but in Persia in 163 B.C. of a mysterious disease. The book of Daniel, therefore, must have been written in about 165 B.C.

Questions for Further Consideration

1. What do you think of the apocalyptic device of recounting history in symbolic and figurative language? Why do you think that the apocalyptic writers chose this method to convey parts of their message?

2. Write your own symbolic history of the period leading up to and including World War II or some other war.

Chapter 12—The Persecution Is Removed

Verses 1-4: "At that time shall arise Michael, the great prince who has charge of your people. And there shall be a time of trouble, such as never has been since there was a nation till that time; but at that time your people shall be delivered, every one whose name shall be found written in the book. And many of those who sleep in the dust of the earth shall awake, some to everlasting life, and some to shame and everlasting contempt. And those who are wise shall shine like the brightness of the firmament; and those who turn many to righteousness, like the stars for ever and ever. But you, Daniel, shut up the words, and seal the book, until the time of the end. Many shall run to and fro, and knowledge shall increase."

These verses conclude the long account begun in chapter 10. And it is here that we find the only reliable reference in the Old Testament to the idea of the resurrection of an individual. The Old Testament writers did not have a developed concept of life after death. The basic Old Testament belief was in the idea of Sheol. This place, located deep within the earth, was where the "lingering personalities" of persons went at the time of death. It was a place of gloom and darkness, where *all* shared the same fate, a bare existence characterized by the weakest kind of life that one can imagine. Rich and poor, good and bad, all shared the same fate at death. This concept was never given up in any of the books of the Old Testament. The only real modification is here in Daniel 12:2.

The passage itself depicts again the great suffering which was to come upon the people of God at the time of Antiochus. Michael, the patron angel of the Jewish people, would protect and help to deliver the people of God who remained faithful. The writer was so certain of this that he could even declare that names were written in a book (presumably this book was in the hands of God). The author then asserted his idea of resurrection. The reader will note immediately that this would *not* be a general resurrection of all to eternal reward or punishment, but rather it would be a resurrection of *some* to life and *some* to shame. The best judgment seems to be that those who would be raised would be those who had died during the period of persecution and who had not received their justly deserved reward or punishment.

Some persons may be misled by the translation "everlasting." "Everlasting" to those of us who stand in the philosophical tradition of the Greeks means "forever, eternal," or something similar. The idea involved in Hebrew thought, however, was that of life in a particular "age." This is the meaning of the Hebrew word used here and which has so often been mistranslated by our term "everlasting." In this case the resurrection would be to life in the coming new age, life free from persecution; within this historical continuum, in this new age the good would be rewarded and the evil punished. We assume that after the accounts were "set straight," the persons would then return to Sheol, the ultimate fate of everyone!

Words of encouragement were given to those who kept the faith (verse 3); they would be the recipients of long life. Daniel was ordered to seal up the words because they were intended for an age long after his own. Again, it is noteworthy that the term used means *not* "end of time" but rather the "time of the end." And the passage repeats that the period spoken about would be a bad time. The best translation of verse 4*b* is not "knowledge shall increase," but rather "disasters shall increase." This is a typical description of the end of an era of persecution and the beginning of a new era in which persecution would be eliminated and those who had been loyal to God would enter a period of peace and happiness.

> Verses 5-13: Then I Daniel looked, and behold, two others stood, one on this bank of the stream and one on that bank of the stream. And I said to the man clothed in linen, who was above the waters of the stream, "How long shall it be till the end of these wonders?" The man clothed in linen, who was above the waters of the stream, raised his right hand and his left hand toward heaven; and I heard him swear by him who lives for ever that it would be for a time, two times, and half a time; and that when the shattering of the power of the holy people comes to an end all these things would be accomplished. I heard, but I did not understand. Then I said, "O my lord, what shall be the issue of these things?" He said, "Go your way, Daniel, for the words are shut up and sealed until the time of the end. Many shall purify themselves, and make themselves white, and be refined; but the wicked shall do wickedly; and none of the wicked shall understand; but those who are wise shall understand. And from the time that the continual burnt offering is taken away, and the abomination that makes desolate is set up, there shall be a thousand two hundred and ninety days. Blessed is he who waits and comes to the thousand three hundred and thirty-five days. But go your way till the end; and you shall rest, and shall stand in your allotted place at the end of the days."

The focus returns to Daniel, with whom the visionary experience had begun (see 10:1 and following). He asked how long it would be before the end of "these wonders"; one of the interpreters answered, ". . . a time, two times, and half a time." The period in which evil flourished was always depicted by the symbolic number 3½. Daniel was assured that these things would not take place until the "time of the end."

In verses 11-12 there is a curious phenomenon: the reader is told that the time from the desecration of the temple would be 1,290 days, approximately 3½ years. This we would expect. But verse 12 mentions a blessing pronounced upon the one who waited and came to the 1,335 days. This new period of time may depict a short interim period between the time that the persecution was ended and such time as things were back to "normal." This may have been the author's way of saying to the faithful that the situation would not miraculously and immediately improve upon the removal of the persecutor. It takes some time for "normalcy" to return; therefore, added patience was needed. Some have even argued that this last verse was a later addition to correct the number of days to the exact number between the desecration of the temple and the actual purification which came after the writer had completed his work. This interpretation seems to be a bit strained, but no really satisfactory solution to this curious figure has yet been postulated!

Summary

The author of Daniel broke some new ground in this last chapter. He postulated a resurrection to life on this earth; it does not seem to be permanent life, however, but only a period of time when the good and bad receive their just deserts. After the period of reward or punishment, things would return to "normal." The author also reiterated his belief that evil was to be allowed to run its course for a definite but limited period of time. When the age of persecution was over, God's people could resume a normal life and worship as they wished.

Questions for Further Consideration

1. Why do you think that only "some" were raised to life in this world, part for reward and part for punishment?

2. What is the essential meaning of this passage in terms of religious implications for a future life?

3. What does the chapter say about the nature of God, evil, and the consequences of personal choice of loyalties in one's life?

Summary of Daniel

The book of Daniel was a summons to people undergoing persecution to keep their religious faith and to refuse to compromise their relationship with God. The author knew that this might well mean martyrdom. He nevertheless urged his people to keep the faith; it was his conviction that there were ultimately greater values to which they should be committed. It was his further conviction that the final hope lay in God, not in the easy road of the moment.

This book, composed as it is of six stories and several apocalyptic visions, was designed to speak to the people of that era. But the religious truths that are contained within these teachings are applicable for any age or any life which finds itself facing similar circumstances.

One final observation should be made here. There are those who feel that to interpret apocalyptic literature in a nonliteral, symbolic manner means that the authors of such books were perpetrating a hoax on their readers. Is it a hoax for a poet to write in poetry? These apocalyptic writers, and Daniel is among them, simply used an accepted literary style of their time as a vehicle for their message. Why should it be a hoax to use such symbols and images? Is it a hoax today to convey certain ideas and messages through political cartoons? Or further, are the parables of Jesus a hoax since these were simply "manufactured" stories told to illustrate and convey religious truths? The fact that these stories were not "historically true" does not take away from their beauty or from the depth of their meaning. Teaching by means of parable was an accepted device then and is still today. Teaching by means of apocalyptic writing was also an accepted practice in those times. The book of Daniel (and later, Revelation) was not intended as a hoax but rather as a proclamation of faith in what the author believed was the one true God. It was a call to the people of God to hold on to that faith in spite of the persecution and hatred of the world.

The Book of Revelation

Introduction

The book known as "Revelation" (*not* Revelations!) is a more complete apocalyptic work than the book of Daniel. But it too has some variations from the usual apocalyptic motifs and characteristics. The book, for example, is not pseudonymous; rather, the author identified himself and was apparently well-known to the readers and hearers of his work. Exactly who this "John" was remains a mystery. From the book itself it appears that he was a church leader who had been exiled for his witness to the faith.

The date of the book is almost universally acknowledged to be about A.D. 95, during the time of persecution which erupted in this part of the empire when Domitian exalted himself to the status of *"Dominus et Deus,"* that is, Lord and God. His insistence on being accorded "divine honors" led to the worship of the emperor and/or the goddess *Roma* with accompanying priesthood and cultus in certain parts of the empire, particularly Asia Minor. The Christians in this area viewed such acts as blasphemy and the command to worship as the most dangerous form of idolatry. Because of this situation many Christians in the area of Asia Minor were being persecuted for their witness to their faith, even to the point of martyrdom. It was in and to this situation that the author of Revelation wrote.

The structure of the book is variously debated by the different commentators, and there seems to be no consensus on a specific outline of the book or the headings for the divisions. There is some consensus on several of the divisions, however, and it is agreed generally that there seems to be a conscious structuring of the book around the number *seven.* Many commentators do indeed attempt to force such a structural scheme too far. I find ten sections in the book and will proceed to interpret the book under the general headings of these ten sections. My outline of the book is as follows:

1. Introduction and Vision of the Son of Man in the Midst of His Church, chapter 1.
2. Letters to the Seven Churches, chapters 2–3.
3. Vision of God and the Lamb, chapters 4–5.
4. Cycle of Judgment: The Seven Seals, chapters 6:1–8:1.
5. Cycle of Judgment: The Seven Trumpets—and Others, chapters 8:2–11:19.
6. Historical Summary, chapters 12–14.
7. Cycle of Judgment: The Seven Bowls of the Wrath of God, chapters 15–16.
8. The Judgment of the Harlot City and the End of the Persecution, chapters 17–20.
9. Vision of the Transformed Age, chapters 21:1–22:5.
10. Epilogue, chapter 22:6-21.

Exposition

1. Chapter 1—Introduction and Vision of the Son of Man in the Midst of His Church

Verses 1-3: The revelation of Jesus Christ, which God gave him to show to his servants what must soon take place; and he made it known by sending his angel to his servant John, who bore witness to the word of God and to the testimony of Jesus Christ, even to all that he saw. Blessed is he who reads aloud the words of the prophecy, and blessed are those who hear, and who keep what is written therein; for the time is near.

These verses constitute the general introduction to the entire work. This "revelation" is the one which Jesus was making known to his servant, John. There is a three-fold blessing (blessings are typical of apocalyptic works) for those who hear and keep what is written therein, and even a blessing upon the one who reads the book aloud (i.e., to the people). It is interesting to note that the author in these three verses had stated *twice* that the "time is near," that these things had to happen "soon." Even though John called this a "prophecy," it was a prophecy in the "true" sense of the word, a message from God for his people. And in such "prophecy" only the immediate future was involved.

Some interpreters are quite confused over whether this book is to be read as prophecy or as an apocalyptic work. It appears that John was simply writing his prophetic message in apocalyptic form. The reader is cautioned not to think of "prophecy" as prediction of the distant future—as popularly but erroneously understood—but as we have defined it above. If these ideas are kept in mind, there will be no confusion about the prophecy/apocalyptic motifs.

Verses 4-8: John to the seven churches that are in Asia: Grace to you and peace from him who is and who was and who is to come, and from the seven spirits who are before his throne, and from Jesus Christ the faithful witness, the firstborn of the dead, and the ruler of kings on earth.

To him who loves us and has freed us from our sins by his blood and made us a kingdom, priests to his God and Father, to him be glory and dominion for ever and ever. Amen. Behold, he is coming with the clouds, and every eye will see him, every one who pierced him; and all tribes of the earth will wail on account of him. Even so, Amen.

"I am the Alpha and the Omega," says the Lord God, who is and who was and who is to come, the Almighty.

John addressed the "seven churches in Asia." It is a fact that there were more than seven churches in Asia, but these seven were probably chosen because the author was familiar with them. And there were *seven* because that would signify for the author the total church. This message was for all the faithful.

We find in verse 4*b* one of the very few trinitarian statements in the entire New Testament: (1) "who is and who was and who is to come" (a better translation of the last phrase would be "is about to act"), that is, God the Father; (2) the seven spirits, meaning the perfect spirit or the Holy Spirit; and (3) Jesus Christ. The description of Jesus was most appropriate for the situation: he was the first born of the dead (martyred); he was ruler of the kings on earth (it was he, not Caesar, who truly ruled); he had freed believers from sin and made of them a kingdom—not a political kingdom but a religious one; they were not kings but priests.

Verse 7 designates a return for the purpose of executing judgment. All the earth stood under his judgment. Verse 8 directs the reader or hearer to the source of power behind Jesus, the Lord God Almighty, the First and the Last.

Verses 9-11: I John, your brother, who share with you in Jesus the tribulation and the kingdom and the patient endurance, was on the island called Patmos on account of the word of God and the testimony of Jesus. I was in the Spirit on the Lord's day, and I heard behind me a loud voice like a trumpet saying, "Write what you see in a book and send it to the seven churches, to Ephesus and to Smyrna and to Pergamum and to Thyatira and to Sardis and to Philadelphia and to Laodicea."

John identified himself and his circumstances. He had been banished to the Isle of Patmos because of his witness to God and Christ. The reference here to the "Lord's Day" is the only reference in the New Testament to "Sunday" as especially holy to the Christians. As with Daniel, John's vision came at the time of worship. He was commanded to write all that he saw in this vision to the seven churches.

Verses 12-20: Then I turned to see the voice that was speaking to me, and on turning I saw seven golden lampstands, and in the midst of the lampstands one like a son of man, clothed with a long robe and with a golden girdle round his breast; his head and his hair were white as white wool, white as snow, his eyes were like a flame of fire, his feet were like burnished bronze, refined as in a furnace, and his voice was like the sound of many waters; in his right hand he held seven stars, from his mouth issued a sharp two-edged sword, and his face was like the sun shining in full strength.

When I saw him, I fell at his feet as though dead. But he laid his right hand upon me, saying, "Fear not, I am the first and the last, and the living one; I died, and behold I am alive for evermore, and I have the keys of Death and Hades. Now write what you see, what is and what is to take place hereafter. As for the mystery of the seven stars which you saw in my right hand, and the seven golden lampstands, the seven stars are the angels of the seven churches and the seven lampstands are the seven churches."

There follows the famous vision of the Son of man in the midst of his church. The people of God could take heart because they were not alone in their suffering. The One who had already conquered the worst that the world had to offer was with them. The vision is not meant to be pictured photographically but rather pictorially as one sees a giant mural which overwhelms the viewer with its magnitude and immensity. It may be that the specific accessories for the Son of man in the vision symbolize different aspects of his being, but there is no real unanimity among commentators about the symbolism. That some was intended seems certain, however. The seven lampstands (a lampstand symbolizes the church) represent the total or complete church which centers on the Son of man (here definitely a reference to Jesus). The symbols are drawn from various parts of the Old Testament: Daniel 7; Ezekiel 1 and 42; Isaiah 6 and 49; Exodus 19 and 34. This author was a master at drawing together symbols taken from many different parts of the Old Testament text. The figure of the Son of man is overwhelming.

As typical in apocalyptic literature, the seer fell down—in a sense, stupefied. The person revealed in the vision identified himself directly. He is the one who has died, yet lives; he has the keys (authority) over death and even the place of the dead (i.e., Hades). It is interesting that the seven lampstands are designated as the seven churches and the seven stars he held in his hand as the guardian angels of these churches.

Summary

The author introduced his readers and hearers to a promise of both suffering and redemption. The faithful can take heart, however, because the God of all things is in control, not the kings of this world. He will *soon* intervene in judgment on the forces of evil. And the Son of man, lord of life, is in the midst of his churches. Therefore, take heart and keep the faith!

Questions for Further Consideration

1. What specific figures and descriptions in this chapter would inspire faith and hope in people who were experiencing persecution for their religious convictions? Why?

2. What do you think the author meant in referring to the expectation that these events would happen *soon*? What does that do to the idea that this book was written to be fulfilled thousands of years in the future?

3. What do you think is the meaning of the Son of man vision?

2. Chapters 2-3—Letters to the Seven Churches

These chapters contain seven letters, one each to the seven churches in Asia already named. These were real churches in existence at that moment of history and do *not* represent church "ages" or "dispensations." In each of the letters a definite pattern was followed: (1) an introduction with certain characteristics of the Son of man drawn from chapter 1; (2) encouragement for the good in the church; (3) criticism for the evil in the church and a warning if the evil was not corrected; (4) an exhortation to right the wrongs and to keep the faith along with a promise of reward for remaining loyal to God. The order of the letters may have been dictated by the order in which the writing would have been delivered. And the author's knowledge of the historical circumstances in these cities was accurate indeed.

Verses 1-7: "To the angel of the church in Ephesus write: 'The words of him who holds the seven stars in his right hand, who walks among the seven golden lampstands.

"'I know your works, your toil and your patient endurance, and how you cannot bear evil men but have tested those who call themselves apostles but are not, and found them to be false; I know you are enduring patiently and bearing up for my name's sake, and you have not grown weary. But I have this against you, that you have abandoned the love you had at first. Remember then from what you have fallen, repent and do the works you did at first. If not, I will come to you and remove your lampstand from its place, unless you repent. Yet this you have, you hate the works of the Nicolaitans, which I also hate. He who has an ear, let him hear what the Spirit says to the churches. To him who conquers I will grant to eat of the tree of life, which is in the paradise of God.'"

The church at Ephesus was commended because, in the midst of bad times, the people there were still zealous to keep their church "pure." They had worked diligently and alertly against those who would weaken the church from within: both those who were evil and posed as "apostles" and those who taught libertine doctrines which led to immoral living (the Nicolaitans). In all their zeal to keep pure, however, the church people evidently became a group of inquisitorial witch-hunters; their motivation lacked the one essential ingredient which makes the church the church—love! And to the "one who conquers" would be given the gift of life.

Verses 8-11: "And to the angel of the church in Smyrna write: 'The words of the first and the last, who died and came to life.

"'I know your tribulation and your poverty (but you are rich) and the slander of those who say that they are Jews and are not, but are a synagogue of Satan. Do not fear what you are about to suffer. Behold, the devil is about to throw some of you into prison, that you may be tested, and for ten days you will have tribulation. Be faithful unto death, and I will give you the crown of life. He who has an ear, let him hear what the Spirit says to the churches. He who conquers shall not be hurt by the second death.'"

The people of the church at Smyrna were in dire straits, suffering both persecution and poverty. The early church often had difficulty with Jewish opposition; obviously the problems here were compounded by such activity. John alerted these people to the very real possibility that they would be thrown into prison, a procedure usually followed by execution. He urged that they not lose their faith even in the face of martyrdom. If they remained loyal, they too would receive the gift of life and would not be hurt by the "second death." This term seems to refer to the ultimate separation of a person from God, and it was the second death which was to be feared, not mere physical death.

Verses 12-17: "And to the angel of the church in Pergamum write: 'The words of him who has the sharp two-edged sword.

"'I know where you dwell, where Satan's throne is; you hold fast my name and you did not deny my faith even in the days of Antipas my witness, my faithful one, who was killed among you, where Satan dwells. But I have a few things against you: you have some there who hold the teaching of Balaam, who taught Balak to put a stumbling block before the sons of Israel, that they might eat food sacrificed to idols and practice immorality. So you also have some who hold the teaching of the Nicolaitans. Repent then. If not, I will come to you soon and war against them with the sword of my mouth. He who has an ear, let him hear what the Spirit says to the churches. To him who conquers I will give some of the hidden manna, and I will give him a white stone, with a new name written on the stone which no one knows except him who receives it.'"

It was in Pergamum, the Roman capital of the province of Asia that the imperial cult began. In 29 B.C. the first temple was built there for the use of the imperial cult; hence the reference to "Satan's throne." That the dangers here were very real is seen in the mention of the martyr death of a certain Antipas. In the face of these pressures there were those ("who hold the teaching of Balaam") who participated in the idolatry of the city, and others (the Nicolaitans) who held that such actions did not really matter anyway! John felt that these were serious offenses which, even though the church was suffering persecution, could not be condoned and thus stood under the judgment of God. To those who conquered would go the reward of eating the "hidden manna," meaning that the faithful ones would eat at the Lord's table in the new age. And further, each one would be given a white stone (probably a sort of "ticket") for admission into the blessings of the new age. The stone was white because it symbolized victory, and it had a new name written on it "which no one knows" as a sign of protection. In the ancient world, to know a person's name was to give the one knowing a certain power over that person. The faithful here would receive a new secret name so that no one except their Lord would have dominion over them.

Verses 18-29: "And to the angel of the church in Thyatira write: 'The words of the Son of God, who has eyes like a flame of fire, and whose feet are like burnished bronze.

"'I know your works, your love and faith and service and patient endurance, and that your latter works exceed the first. But I have this against you, that you tolerate the woman Jezebel, who calls herself a prophetess and is teaching and beguiling my servants to practice immorality and to eat food sacrificed to idols. I gave her time to repent, but she refuses to repent of her immorality. Behold, I will throw her on a sickbed, and those who commit adultery with her I will throw into great tribulation, unless they repent of her doings; and I will strike her children dead. And all the churches shall know that I am he who searches mind and heart, and I will give to each of you as your works deserve. But to the rest of you in Thyatira, who do not hold this teaching, who have not learned what some call the deep things of Satan, to you I say, I do not lay upon you any other burden; only hold fast what you have, until I come. He who conquers and who keeps my works until the end, I will give him power over the nations, and he shall rule them with a rod of iron, as when earthen pots are broken in pieces, even as I myself have received power from my Father; and I will give him the morning star. He who has an ear, let him hear what the Spirit says to the churches.'"

The church in Thyatira had much to commend it. It had retained "love and faith and service and patient endurance" where some other churches had not. Yet the same kind of internal threat was present here as well. Exactly who the woman "Jezebel" was is not known, but what *is* known is that she was obviously advocating the same type of intellectualism and immorality that was being espoused by the Nicolaitans in other churches. As with the Jezebel of the past, she was attempting to lead God's people into idolatry. But John's conviction was that those who followed such teaching and shared such apostasy would be judged rather severely (verse 27). This judgment would be directly linked to the witness of those who held the true faith until the end. The one who remained faithful would receive the "morning star." This was a reference to Christ, or possibly, but less probably, the resurrection.

Chapter 3:1-6: "And to the angel of the church in Sardis write: 'The words of him who has the seven spirits of God and the seven stars.

"'I know your works; you have the name of being alive, and you are dead. Awake, and strengthen what remains and is on the point of death, for I have not found your works perfect in the sight of my God. Remember then what you received and heard; keep that, and repent. If you will not awake, I will come like a thief, and you will not know at what hour I will come upon you. Yet you have still a few names in Sardis, people who have not soiled their garments; and they shall walk with me in white, for they are worthy. He who conquers shall be clad thus in white garments, and I will not blot his name out of the book of life; I will confess his name before my Father and before his angels. He who has an ear, let him hear what the Spirit says to the churches.'"

In contrast to the other churches so far addressed, Sardis had no problems. It had no martyr threat from without nor internal dissension within. It was a church that looked alive but was dead! Their works were not completed—they began but did not finish. If they remained asleep, the judgment would come swift and certain (as it did to the city of Sardis in about 546 and 218 B.C. when the city became too complacent and thus lax in its watchfulness). There were a few who still remained faithful; their names would remain in the book of life (a book which listed the names of the citizens of a city, in this case the city was the new Jerusalem). It is interesting to note that one's name could be blotted out of this book. Whether one remained in or was blotted out, however, lay in the hands of the individual. Only that person—not Caesar, not Satan, not evil, not one's enemies—had the power to remove one's name from the book of life!

Verses 7-13: "And to the angel of the church in Philadelphia write: 'The words of the holy one, the true one, who has the key of David, who opens and no one shall shut, who shuts and no one opens.

"'I know your works. Behold, I have set before you an open door, which no one is able to shut; I know that you have but little power, and yet you have kept my word and have not denied my name. Behold, I will make those of the synagogue of Satan who say that they are Jews and are not, but lie—behold, I will make them come and bow down before your feet, and learn that I have loved you. Because you have kept my word of patient endurance, I will keep you from the hour of trial which is coming on the whole world, to try those who dwell upon the earth. I am coming soon; hold fast what you have, so that no one may seize your crown. He who conquers, I will make him a pillar in the temple of my God; never shall he go out of it, and I will write on him the name of my God, and the name of the city of my God, the new Jerusalem which comes down from my God out of heaven, and my own new name. He who has an ear, let him hear what the Spirit says to the churches.'"

The Philadelphians were having much the same trouble as the people at Smyrna, Their problem was basically from the Jewish community which was making trouble for them. They were promised that the judgment on the persecutors was to come *soon*. The reference to the "pillar in the temple of God" reflected the strong conviction that for those who "keep the faith" there could never be a time when they would be absent from the very presence of God.

Verses 14-22: "And to the angel of the church in Laodicea write: 'The words of the Amen, the faithful and true witness, the beginning of God's creation.

"'I know your works: you are neither cold nor hot. Would that you were cold or hot! So, because you are lukewarm, and neither cold nor hot, I will spew you out of my mouth. For you say, I am rich, I have prospered, and I need nothing; not knowing that you are wretched, pitiable, poor, blind, and naked. Therefore I counsel you to buy from me gold refined by fire, that you may be rich, and white garments to clothe you and to keep the shame of your nakedness from being seen, and salve to anoint your eyes, that you may see. Those whom I love, I reprove and chasten; so be zealous and repent. Behold, I stand at the door and knock; if any one hears my voice and opens the door, I will come in to him and eat with him, and he with me. He who conquers, I will grant him to sit with me on my throne, as I myself conquered and sat down with my Father on his throne. He who has an ear, let him hear what the Spirit says to the churches.'"

Laodicea was a very rich and progressive city, possessing a great reputation for medicinal salve, fine cloth, a renowned medical school, and prosperous banking and commercial enterprises. In such a setting many people felt that "all's right with the world," so, why worry! This attitude had permeated the thinking of the church as well, and John had strong words for such an attitude. He emphasized that real wealth, real clothing, and real "seeing" were all much deeper than viewed by the standards of the world. And in such a situation failure to choose definitely one way or the other was inexcusable. In verse 20 the well-known figure of Jesus standing at the door and knocking is a marvelous symbol by the writer of Revelation. Jesus is knocking on the door of his church, however, not the door to the individual's heart! The church can lock him out of his own institution. There is hope for those individuals who hear him, for he promises to be with all those who desire fellowship with him. And the reward is sure as is the suffering. The one who conquers is obviously the one who holds to the faith in spite of the consequences.

Summary

There are some commentators who maintain that verses 20-22 are not the conclusion to the letter to Laodicea but, in reality, constitute a fitting summary and challenge for all the seven letters. It is possible that this hypothesis is correct, but it violates the pattern which we have seen in each of the other letters. It is more probable that each letter is "self-contained"; this is not to say, however, that each letter was meant only for one church. The challenge at the conclusion of each letter was addressed to the *churches,* not simply the single church. All the churches and people of God—present and future—are represented in these letters, both in the commendations for right conduct and in the warnings and admonitions about false doctrine, immoral living, and unfaithfulness to the Lord of life! Persecution is no excuse for failing to witness to the faith; it just makes such a witness more difficult.

There are some interpretations of these two chapters which find in these seven letters a symbolic representation of the history of the church. Church history is divided in these schemes into seven "church ages" or "dispensations," the first being "almost perfect" and the others in succession becoming more and more evil until the last age finds the church extremely corrupt, so much so that it is "spewed out." At this point Jesus returns to judge the world and establish his kingdom. This type of interpretation is called "dispensationalism," and there are varieties of this kind of interpretation.

It is clear, however, from a close examination of these chapters that no such intention was in the mind of the author. First of all, he addressed each letter not simply to one church but to all the churches. Secondly, it is simply not true that he listed the various churches in a descending order of degeneracy. Thirdly, it is not true that the early church was "nearly perfect"; a careful reading of Acts and First Corinthians will put that myth to rest rather quickly. And fourthly, this kind of interpretation would contradict every other New Testament teaching about the work of the church and the activity of God's Spirit within the church. Jesus' parables depicted a good progressive growth of his followers, even indicating that God's Spirit would lead the church into all the truth. So the accepted and expected path for the church was that of positive growth, not progressive degeneracy.

It is interesting that several denominations have in fact labeled dispensationalism as "heresy." It is clear that no such ideas are incorporated into the text of Revelation!

Questions for Further Consideration

Examine each of the seven letters carefully. What strengths and weaknesses do you find in these churches that are still present today? What about one's own church? One's own life?

3. Chapters 4–5—Vision of God and the Lamb

Verse 1: After this I looked, and lo, in heaven an open door! And the first voice, which I had heard speaking to me like a trumpet, said, "Come up hither, and I will show you what must take place after this."

With chapter 4 the author began his apocalyptic work in earnest with visions, wild symbolism, and interpreters. The two chapters here are really foundational for the remainder of the book; the author believed that the church could keep the faith since it was the God who was revealed in these chapters who rules forever and who would be with them in their suffering!

Verses 2-11: At once I was in the Spirit, and lo, a throne stood in heaven, with one seated on the throne! And he who sat there appeared like jasper and carnelian, and round the throne was a rainbow that looked like an emerald. Round the throne were twenty-four thrones, and seated on the thrones were twenty-four elders, clad in white garments, with golden crowns upon their heads. From the throne issue flashes of lightning, and voices and peals of thunder, and before the throne burn seven torches of fire, which are the seven spirits of God; and before the throne there is as it were a sea of glass, like crystal.

And round the throne, on each side of the throne, are four living creatures, full of eyes in front and behind: the first living creature like a lion, the second living creature like an ox, the third living creature with the face of a man, and the fourth living creature like a flying eagle. And the four living creatures, each of them with six wings, are full of eyes all round and within, and day and night they never cease to sing,

"Holy, holy, holy, is the Lord God
Almighty,
who was and is and is to come!"

And whenever the living creatures give glory and honor and thanks to him who is seated on the throne, who lives for ever and ever, the twenty-four elders fall down before him who is seated on the throne and worship him who lives for ever and ever; they cast their crowns before the throne, singing,

"Worthy art thou, our Lord and God,
to receive glory and honor and power,
for thou didst create all things,
and by thy will they existed and were created."

The author gave a symbolic representation of the presence and majesty of the God of the church. The splendor and awesomeness of the scene is enhanced by the use of precious stones, and the rainbow not only adds to the brightness of the setting but also emphasizes that this God is the God of the promise and the covenant.

There is a great deal of uncertainty about whom the twenty-four elders represent, but it seems clear that the number, 24, being 2 x 12, would most likely represent the Israel of God, both the old and the new. The seven torches probably represent the Holy Spirit. Another element adding to the splendor of the vision is the "sea of glass" before the throne. Again, scholars argue over the exact meaning of the figure, but it probably is no more than another way of enhancing the spectacular appearance of the vision; after all, a great glassy sea would reflect all the brilliance of the throne and magnify that splendor greatly.

The figure of the four living creatures is taken from Ezekiel. Here in Revelation each creature has only one face whereas in Ezekiel each creature has four faces. The number four probably represents the created order; these four representatives from nature were considered to be the most powerful and intelligent. In all probability the meaning is that God's glory is at least partially supported and pointed to by his created order. It is interesting that John did not quote the Old Testament directly but used all kinds of symbols and images drawn from the Old Testament. Even though the living creatures are drawn primarily from Ezekiel 1, they also have six wings, a figure taken from Isaiah 6, and the images are blended together here.

The main duty of all those around the throne was to worship and praise God. They never ceased singing, "Holy, Holy, Holy, . . ." and they worshiped God not simply because he is powerful but because he is more than powerful. He is a God who wishes the best for his created order and who wishes to enter into fellowship and communion with all.

5:1-12: And I saw in the right hand of him who was seated on the throne a scroll written within and on the back, sealed with seven seals; and I saw a strong angel proclaiming with a loud voice, "Who is worthy to open the scroll and break its seals?" And no one in heaven or on earth or under the earth was able to open the scroll or to look into it, and I wept much that no one was found worthy to open the scroll or to look into it. Then one of the elders said to me, "Weep not; lo, the Lion of the tribe of Judah, the Root of David, has conquered, so that he can open the scroll and its seven seals."

And between the throne and the four living creatures and among the elders, I saw a Lamb standing, as though it had been slain, with seven horns and with seven eyes, which are the seven spirits of God sent out into all the earth; and he went and took the scroll from the right hand of him who was seated on the throne. And when he had taken the scroll, the four living creatures and the twenty-four elders fell down before the Lamb, each holding a harp, and with golden bowls full of incense, which are the prayers of the saints; and they sang a new song, saying,

> "Worthy art thou to take the scroll
>   and to open its seals,
> for thou wast slain and by thy blood
>   didst ransom men for God
> from every tribe and tongue and
>   people and nation,
> and hast made them a kingdom and
>   priests to our God,
> and they shall reign on earth."

Then I looked, and I heard around the throne and the living creatures and the elders the voice of many angels, numbering myriads of myriads and thousands of thousands, saying with a loud voice, "Worthy is the Lamb who was slain, to receive power and wealth and wisdom and might and honor and glory and blessing!"

The focus of the vision has shifted to another figure. This is accomplished by focusing on the scroll, sealed with seven seals, in the hand of God. It is interesting that God was not the one who was to open the scroll, but rather someone who was "worthy" must be found. But no one was. The scroll contained much for it was written on both sides; ordinarily only one side of a scroll was used. Exactly what was contained in the scroll is debated by commentators, but upon examination of what happened when the scroll was opened, it seems best to say that the scroll contained the revelation of what was to take place *soon*. In other words, it contained the symbolic representation of the judgment of God upon the forces of evil which were persecuting the people of God.

John wept because no one worthy was found to open the scroll, but he was told that the Lion of the tribe of Judah (a designation of the Messiah) had conquered and would open the scroll. But when John looked into the midst of the throne scene, he saw not a lion but a lamb—and a lamb with "the marks of slaughter on him" (NEB)! In spite of the fact that he had been killed, the Lamb *stood* and had seven horns (complete power) and seven eyes (complete wisdom and knowledge). This is one of the most meaningful symbols in the book of Revelation. The world judges on the basis of power and strength; but real power and strength lie in other directions. To those who were undergoing persecution, facing possible death, the figure of the Lamb who had been killed and yet stood would rekindle in their hearts the belief that God's ways are not human ways, and his values are beyond human values. The evil of this world does *not* have the final word!

There is, of course, no question as to the identity of the Lamb. It is Jesus, the Lord of the church, the one who holds the keys to death and the place of death. When He took the scroll from God, the scene again reverberated with a hymn of praise, this one in honor of the Lamb.

Verses 13-14: And I heard every creature in heaven and on earth and under the earth and in the sea, and all therein, saying, "To him who sits upon the throne and the Lamb be blessing and honor and glory and might for ever and ever!" And the four living creatures said, "Amen!" and the elders fell down and worshiped.

The conclusion of the vision comes with a crescendo of praise not only from those around the throne but also from all creatures everywhere who ascribe praise to God and the Lamb.

Summary

Chapters 4 and 5 of Revelation contain a magnificent and breathtaking scene in which God and the Lamb receive the praise and honor due to them. But these chapters are sources of hope to the persecuted, for through these symbols the message is loud and clear: God reigns and will execute his justice upon those who attempt to pervert and corrupt his created order!

Questions for Further Consideration

1. Examine the symbolism of these chapters carefully. What are the most significant symbols and images? Why? What do they mean?

2. How do these chapters set the stage for the remainder of the book?

4. Chapters 6:1–8:1—Cycle of Judgment: The Seven Seals

6:1-8: Now I saw when the Lamb opened one of the seven seals, and I heard one of the four living creatures say, as with a voice of thunder, "Come!" And I saw, and behold, a white horse, and its rider had a bow; and a crown was given to him, and he went out conquering and to conquer.

When he opened the second seal, I heard the second living creature say, "Come!" And out came another horse, bright red; its rider was permitted to take peace from the earth, so that men should slay one another; and he was given a great sword.

When he opened the third seal, I heard the third living creature say, "Come!" And I saw, and behold, a black horse, and its rider had a balance in his hand; and I heard what seemed to be a voice in the midst of the four living creatures saying, "A quart of wheat for a denarius, and three quarts of barley for a denarius; but do not harm oil and wine!"

When he opened the fourth seal, I heard the voice of the fourth living creature say, "Come!" And I saw, and behold, a pale horse, and its rider's name was Death, and Hades followed him; and they were given power over a fourth of the earth, to kill with sword and with famine and with pestilence and by wild beasts of the earth.

The cycles of judgment begin with the opening of the seals. The Four Horsemen of the Apocalypse are famous, but in reality these should be viewed as a unit and not as separate entities. In this sequence it is the color which gives the symbolism direction. White is the symbol of victory; thus, the rider on the white horse is a conqueror whose avowed purpose is to conquer for the sake of conquering. When such an attitude or activity is begun, it sets off a cycle of events that run a course eventuating in death. The red horse is war; the black horse is famine and want; the pale (or "greenish-gray") horse is death. One of John's favorite ideas was that evil is self-destructive; this is the point of the cycle of the horsemen. God does not intervene here; the steps fall naturally into order and those whose sole purpose is to impose their will on all others will be led into the jaws of death. In the process, unfortunately, innocent persons will also suffer because of these evil acts.

Verses 9-11: When he opened the fifth seal, I saw under the altar the souls of those who had been slain for the word of God and for the witness they had borne; they cried out with a loud voice, "O Sovereign Lord, holy and true, how long before thou wilt judge and avenge our blood on those who dwell upon the earth?" Then they were each given a white robe and told to rest a little longer, until the number of their fellow servants and their brethren should be complete, who were to be killed as they themselves had been.

This leads us to the fifth seal where the martyrs are seen under the heavenly altar crying, "How long?" Many find here a note of vengeance which is out of character with the usual Christian doctrine of forgiveness of one's enemies. To interpret the passage in that manner is to miss the point, however, because the cry was not for personal vengeance but for *God's* justice to be active. If God allowed the martyrs to be slain without any sign that they were right, that would vindicate the persecutor and invalidate the martyrs' faith. So it was not vengeance that was requested but justice, not individual vindication but the vindication of God's promise. Each martyr was given a white robe, a symbol of victory, and told that evil would be allowed to run its course—but no more than that! They were also told that the number of martyrs was not yet complete, thus indicating to the people of the church that the worst was not yet over.

Verses 12-17: When he opened the sixth seal, I looked, and behold, there was a great earthquake; and the sun became black as sackcloth, the full moon became like blood, and the stars of the sky fell to the earth as the fig tree sheds its winter fruit when shaken by a gale; the sky vanished like a scroll that is rolled up, and every mountain and island was removed from its place. Then the kings of the earth and the great men and the generals and the rich and the strong, and every one, slave and free, hid in the caves and among the rocks of the mountains, calling to the mountains and rocks, "Fall on us and hide us from the face of him who is seated on the throne, and from the wrath of the Lamb; for the great day of their wrath has come, and who can stand before it?"

With the opening of the sixth seal there is a typical apocalyptic scene in which all sorts of natural phenomena are depicted to show that judgment is a serious matter and is not limited to one time or one place. Evil is worldwide; so is judgment. The reader is at this point prepared for the final act, but it does not come. Instead John provided an interlude which involved the "sealing" of God's people.

7:1-8: After this I saw four angels standing at the four corners of the earth, holding back the four winds of the earth, that no wind might

blow on earth or sea or against any tree. Then I saw another angel
ascend from the rising of the sun, with the seal of the living God,
and he called with a loud voice to the four angels who had been
given power to harm earth and sea, saying, "Do not harm the earth
or the sea or the trees, till we have sealed the servants of our God
upon their foreheads." And I heard the number of the sealed, a
hundred and forty-four thousand sealed, out of every tribe of the
sons of Israel, twelve thousand sealed out of the tribe of Judah,
twelve thousand of the tribe of Reuben, twelve thousand of the
tribe of Gad, twelve thousand of the tribe of Asher, twelve
thousand of the tribe of Naphtali, twelve thousand of the tribe of
Manasseh, twelve thousand of the tribe of Simeon, twelve
thousand of the tribe of Levi, twelve thousand of the tribe of
Issachar, twelve thousand of the tribe of Zebulun, twelve thousand of the tribe of Joseph, twelve thousand sealed out of the tribe
of Benjamin.

Most apocalyptic works exhibit the teaching that when God
executes his judgment on the evil of this world, the people of God are
afforded a special kind of protection. After all, they are part of the
world order, and it would be impossible for calamity to befall a place,
small or large, and not affect the righteous. Therefore, there were
various solutions among the apocalyptic writers for this kind of
situation. Some of them urged the people of God to be alert to the
signs of impending danger; when these appeared, they were to beat a
hasty exit (see Mark 13:14-19 and parallels). Others expected a kind
of interlude between the persecution and the final judgment wherein
the people of God could enjoy a period of calm and freedom from
persecution, a type of "interim" kingdom (see IV Ezra 7:25ff.). Still
others taught that the times would be so terrible that God's people
would suffer along with others even though the judgment was not
directed at them; therefore, some believed that the time of suffering
would be shortened (see Mark 13:20 where this motif is connected
with the first discussed above) for the sake of God's elect.

What the reader finds at this point in Revelation is similar to this
last motif. The judgment was expected and would come upon those
who deserved it. What about those who had been faithful to God and
to his Christ? The judgment was to be delayed (see verses 1-3) until the
people of God were "sealed." The "seal" was a sign that these people
were to be afforded special protection in the ensuing period of
judgment on evil. The number was, of course, symbolic, representing
the total number of the people of God. There were twelve thousand

$(12 \times 10^3$, 12 being the number of people of God and 10 being the number denoting completeness, raised to the third power) from each of the twelve tribes, i.e., the people of God.

7:9–8:1: After this I looked, and behold, a great multitude which no man could number, from every nation, from all tribes and peoples and tongues, standing before the throne and before the Lamb, clothed in white robes, with palm branches in their hands, and crying out with a loud voice, "Salvation belongs to our God who sits upon the throne, and to the Lamb!" And all the angels stood round the throne and round the elders and the four living creatures, and they fell on their faces before the throne and worshiped God, saying, "Amen! Blessing and glory and wisdom and thanksgiving and honor and power and might be to our God for ever and ever! Amen."

Then one of the elders addressed me, saying, "Who are these, clothed in white robes, and whence have they come?" I said to him, "Sir, you know." And he said to me, "These are they who have come out of the great tribulation; they have washed their robes and made them white in the blood of the Lamb.

> Therefore are they before the throne of God,
>   and serve him day and night within his temple;
>   and he who sits upon the throne
>   will shelter them with his presence.
> They shall hunger no more, neither
>   thirst any more;
>   the sun shall not strike them, nor
>   any scorching heat.
> For the Lamb in the midst of the
>   throne will be their shepherd,
>   and he will guide them to springs
>   of living water;
>   and God will wipe away every tear
>   from their eyes."

When the Lamb opened the seventh seal, there was silence in heaven for about half an hour.

The focus shifts back to the throne vision of chapters 4-5. The seer observed a huge number from every part of the entire world standing, clothed in the garb of victory, before the throne in a great scene of adoration and worship to God and the Lamb. The identity of those clothed in white was made known; these were the faithful martyrs (probably to be understood as coming from all generations of human existence) who had kept the faith in the face of such evil. Then the seventh seal was opened and there was total silence for a short while. The dramatic qualities of the writing can be seen clearly here!

Questions for Further Consideration

1. The teaching in the cycle of the "four horsemen" about judgment on sin is that evil is self-destructive. What kinds of examples can you think of in contemporary times, in terms of both institutions and individual persons, that demonstrate the truth of this teaching?

2. Is the cry of the martyrs justified? Why or why not? Can you think of any situations within the past half-century that could correspond to the historical setting of the writer of Revelation?

3. When judgment does fall on evil, the people of God can be hurt also. Can you think of times when this has happened or when the time of evil was mercifully shortened?

5. Chapter 8:2—11:19—Cycle of Judgment: The Seven Trumpets, and Others

8:2-6: Then I saw the seven angels who stand before God, and seven trumpets were given to them. And another angel came and stood at the altar with a golden censer; and he was given much incense to mingle with the prayers of all the saints upon the golden altar before the throne; and the smoke of the incense rose with the prayers of the saints from the hand of the angel before God. Then the angel took the censer and filled it with fire from the altar and threw it on the earth; and there were peals of thunder, voices, flashes of lightning, and an earthquake.

Now the seven angels who had the seven trumpets made ready to blow them.

Instead of a final scene of destruction and judgment upon the enemies of God and his people, the author wrote of a new series of judgments in a new cycle, the seven trumpets.

Verses 7-13: The first angel blew his trumpet, and there followed hail and fire, mixed with blood, which fell on the earth; and a third of the earth was burnt up, and a third of the trees were burnt up, and all green grass was burnt up.

The second angel blew his trumpet, and something like a great mountain, burning with fire, was thrown into the sea; and a third of the sea became blood, a third of the living creatures in the sea died, and a third of the ships were destroyed.

The third angel blew his trumpet, and a great star fell from heaven, blazing like a torch, and it fell on a third of the rivers and on the fountains of water. The name of the star is Wormwood. A third of the waters became wormwood, and many men died of the water, because it was made bitter.

The fourth angel blew his trumpet, and a third of the sun was struck, and a third of the moon, and a third of the stars, so that a third of their light was darkened; a third of the day was kept from shining, and likewise a third of the night.

Then I looked, and I heard an eagle crying with a loud voice, as it flew in midheaven, "Woe, woe, woe to those who dwell on the earth, at the blasts of the other trumpets which the three angels are about to blow!"

The first four trumpets, like the first four seals, are directly tied to the earth and to judgment upon the earth for the evils of the old age.

But with the seals, judgment follows a natural sequence since evil is depicted as self-destructive; with the trumpets, God himself takes an active and more direct role. The judgment here fell within the natural order which was directly ruled by God. The scene is quite reminiscent of the plagues in Egypt. Again the judgment was partial; only one-third of the items struck were destroyed. That these episodes were to be taken symbolically is obvious, for how could one-third of the sun be taken away or one-third of the moon in such a way that a third of the day or night be "kept from shining"? Incidentally, the Greek word usually translated "eagle" would best be translated here as "vulture," since the vulture circling is truly an ominous sign!

9:1-12: And the fifth angel blew his trumpet, and I saw a star fallen from heaven to earth, and he was given the key of the shaft of the bottomless pit; he opened the shaft of the bottomless pit, and from the shaft rose smoke like the smoke of a great furnace, and the sun and the air were darkened with the smoke from the shaft. Then from the smoke came locusts on the earth, and they were given power like the power of scorpions of the earth; they were told not to harm the grass of the earth or any green growth or any tree, but only those of mankind who have not the seal of God upon their foreheads; they were allowed to torture them for five months, but not to kill them, and their torture was like the torture of a scorpion, when it stings a man. And in those days men will seek death and will not find it; they will long to die, and death will fly from them.

In appearance the locusts were like horses arrayed for battle; on their heads were what looked like crowns of gold; their faces were like human faces, their hair like women's hair, and their teeth like lions' teeth; they had scales like iron breastplates, and the noise of their wings was like the noise of many chariots with horses rushing into battle. They have tails like scorpions, and stings, and their power of hurting men for five months lies in their tails. They have as king over them the angel of the bottomless pit; his name in Hebrew is Abaddon, and in Greek he is called Apollyon.

The first woe has passed; behold, two woes are still to come.

With the fifth seal the reader is shown that evil is greater than the sum of its parts, for with the opening of the bottomless pit (here a symbol for the accumulated power of the forces of evil) horrible creatures were unleashed on the earth. For five months they were allowed to torture (not kill) persons who did not have the seal of God. The number 5 is interesting and puzzling since 5 is not a typical apocalyptic number; it may be a reference to the five-month span when locusts appeared in that part of the world. It probably means a short period of time, a period longer than 3½ years, the period in which the righteous of God always suffered.

The description of these locust-like creatures is frightening indeed. It is clear that these monsters were not a "happenstance" group, each inflicting harm as it could, but rather constituted a well-organized, well-disciplined army with a leader whose name was "Destroyer." These hideous monsters inflicted suffering, but it is significant that they had human faces. Sin and evil could not exist apart from human beings. This figure was perhaps John's way of pointing out that evil reaches monstrous proportions because of and by means of human sin. (There is absolutely no truth in the interpretation that sees here a prediction of helicopters!)

Verses 13-21: Then the sixth angel blew his trumpet, and I heard a voice from the four horns of the golden altar before God, saying to the sixth angel who had the trumpet, "Release the four angels who are bound at the great river Euphrates." So the four angels were released, who had been held ready for the hour, the day, the month, and the year, to kill a third of mankind. The number of the troops of cavalry was twice ten thousand times ten thousand; I heard their number. And this was how I saw the horses in my vision: the riders wore breastplates the color of fire and of sapphire and of sulphur, and the heads of the horses were like lions' heads, and fire and smoke and sulphur issued from their mouths. By these three plagues a third of mankind was killed, by the fire and smoke and sulphur issuing from their mouths. For the power of the horses is in their mouths and in their tails; their tails are like serpents, with heads, and by means of them they wound.

The rest of mankind, who were not killed by these plagues, did not repent of the works of their hands nor give up worshiping demons and idols of gold and silver and bronze and stone and wood, which cannot either see or hear or walk; nor did they repent of their murders or their sorceries or their immorality or their thefts.

The next trumpet released a multitude of cavalry, this time for the purpose of killing one-third of humankind. These horsemen were also monstrous in appearance; the horses themselves were like nothing ever seen in nature.

The main point here, however, is found in verses 20-21. Judgment had fallen on wicked humanity, but it was a partial judgment. It had as its goal the sole purpose of repentance for those who were left. Evil, however, did not surrender so easily. Rather than causing people to open their eyes and turn to the God of truth and love, these judgments resulted in their being even more hardened in their commitment to the worshiping of idols, which ultimately could be traced to a worship of themselves!

10:1-7: Then I saw another mighty angel coming down from heaven, wrapped in a cloud, with a rainbow over his head, and his face was like the sun, and his legs like pillars of fire. He had a little scroll open in his hand. And he set his right foot on the sea, and his left foot on the land, and called out with a loud voice, like a lion roaring; when he called out, the seven thunders sounded. And when the seven thunders had sounded, I was about to write, but I heard a voice from heaven saying, "Seal up what the seven thunders have said, and do not write it down." And the angel whom I saw standing on sea and land lifted up his right hand to heaven and swore by him who lives for ever and ever, who created heaven and what is in it, the earth and what is in it, and the sea and what is in it, that there should be no more delay, but that in the days of the trumpet call to be sounded by the seventh angel, the mystery of God, as he announced to his servants the prophets, should be fulfilled.

Another angel appeared in the interlude between the sixth and seventh parts of the cycle. This angel is depicted in magnificent terms and showed to John a new cycle of judgment, the seven thunders. But John was commanded to set aside the seven thunders and not to write them down. Various interpretations of this curious act have been given, but the explanation probably lies in verse 6. Here John was told that there would be "no more delay." The seven thunders were bypassed to shorten the days of suffering for the sake of God's people. We have already mentioned that this was a typical apocalyptic device (see Mark 13:20).

Verses 8-11: Then the voice which I had heard from heaven spoke to me again, saying, "Go, take the scroll which is open in the hand of the angel who is standing on the sea and on the land." So I went to the angel and told him to give me the little scroll; and he said to me, "Take it and eat; it will be bitter to your stomach, but sweet as honey in your mouth." And I took the little scroll from the hand of the angel and ate it; it was sweet as honey in my mouth, but when I had eaten it my stomach was made bitter. And I was told, "You must again prophesy about many peoples and nations and tongues and kings."

John was told to take a "little scroll" from the angel and to eat it. This type of command was not unknown to the prophets of God (see Ezekiel 3:1-3; also Jeremiah 15:6). The word of God was sweet to the taste, but the content of the message could be painful indeed to the stomach. It was given to John to proclaim, as the prophets of old had proclaimed, the message of God's judgment upon the evil of this world.

11:1-2: Then I was given a measuring rod like a staff, and I was told: "Rise and measure the temple of God and the altar and those who worship there, but do not measure the court outside the temple; leave that out, for it is given over to the nations, and they will trample over the holy city for forty-two months."

John was told to measure the temple and the people who worshiped there. Measuring is a symbol for one of two things: judgment or safety. In this case it is the latter that is intended. The idea of allowing only the outer court to be trampled is probably a way of indicating both the ultimate security of the faithful and the fact that the faithful would experience great hardship and persecution for forty-two months (3½ years).

Verses 3-6: "And I will grant my two witnesses power to prophesy for one thousand two hundred and sixty days, clothed in sackcloth."
These are the two olive trees and the two lampstands which stand before the Lord of the earth. And if any one would harm them, fire pours from their mouth and consumes their foes; if any one would harm them, thus he is doomed to be killed. They have power to shut the sky, that no rain may fall during the days of their prophesying, and they have power over the waters to turn them into blood, and to smite the earth with every plague, as often as they desire.

At the same time (i.e., 1,260 days = 3½ years) God made it possible for his two witnesses to speak for him during the period of suffering. The two were, of course, symbolic. The lampstand and the olive trees refer to an illustration from Zechariah where the two witnesses are

Zerubbabel and Joshua; here, John identified them with Elijah (no rain, verse 6*a*) and Moses (the plagues, verse 6*b*). However else one wishes to interpret the identity of these witnesses, it is clear that symbolically they represent the church witnessing to the Law and the Prophets, God's revelation, in the time of persecution. The idea is that in spite of the travesty of normal existence at this time, the church and its members can still bear witness against the world.

> Verses 7-14: And when they have finished their testimony, the beast that ascends from the bottomless pit will make war upon them and conquer them and kill them, and their dead bodies will lie in the street of the great city which is allegorically called Sodom and Egypt, where their Lord was crucified. For three days and a half men from the peoples and tribes and tongues and nations gaze at their dead bodies and refuse to let them be placed in a tomb, and those who dwell on the earth will rejoice over them and make merry and exchange presents, because these two prophets had been a torment to those who dwell on the earth. But after the three and a half days a breath of life from God entered them, and they stood up on their feet, and great fear fell on those who saw them. Then they heard a loud voice from heaven saying to them, "Come up hither!" And in the sight of their foes they went up to heaven in a cloud. And at that hour there was a great earthquake, and a tenth of the city fell; seven thousand people were killed in the earthquake, and the rest were terrified and gave glory to the God of heaven.
> The second woe has passed; behold, the third woe is soon to come.

The two witnesses were slain by the beast that ascended from the bottomless pit, the symbolic representation of evil and all those forces whose avowed will and purpose it was to establish a new order of authority and power.

The witnesses lay unburied (a horrible insult in the ancient world) in the streets of the "great city." The identity of this city is debated by commentators, but the city is probably Rome. The term "great city" is a designation for Rome at every other place in the book of Revelation. The symbolism of Sodom and Egypt is clear enough: they represent gross immorality and slavery (to sin). These two were the basic components which led to the crucifixion of Jesus.

For 3½ days the bodies lay in the streets while the people on earth ". . . rejoice and make merry and exchange presents . . ." because of their deaths. The revelation of God (the Law and the Prophets) was a grave nuisance to the world and the servants of evil. But after the 3½ days the two witnesses came to life again; when they did, an earthquake occurred which killed seven thousand persons, again a partial (even though substantial) judgment. When this happened, there were some who were awestruck and gave glory to God. There was still hope for some people of the world because of the witness of the church and because it survived in spite of all the worst that the world could do.

Verses 15-19: Then the seventh angel blew his trumpet, and there were loud voices in heaven, saying, "The kingdom of the world has become the kingdom of our Lord and of his Christ, and he shall reign for ever and ever." And the twenty-four elders who sit on their thrones before God fell on their faces and worshiped God, saying,

> "We give thanks to thee, Lord God
>   Almighty, who art and who wast,
>   that thou hast taken thy great
>   power and begun to reign.
> The nations raged, but thy wrath
>   came,
>   and the time for the dead to be
>   judged,
> for rewarding thy servants, the
>   prophets and saints,
>   and those who fear thy name,
>   both small and great,
>   and for destroying the destroyers of
>   the earth."

Then God's temple in heaven was opened, and the ark of his covenant was seen within his temple; and there were flashes of lightning, voices, peals of thunder, an earthquake, and heavy hail.

The seventh trumpet was blown, and the scene shifts again to heaven where another scene of worship is depicted. Even though the final acts had not yet been concluded, nevertheless, the hosts of heaven could say with authority and hope for the people of God that indeed, "The kingdom of the world has [already] become the kingdom of our Lord and of his Christ, and he shall reign for ever and ever."

Summary

For those who wish to find a strict chronological progression in the book of Revelation, frustration is compounded! The book seems to build to a climax only to have new cycles or additional episodes inserted at the very point when it seems that nothing else should transpire. The author of Revelation, while understanding that there is basically an historical progression in the development of the world of human experience, also understood that the world is a complex and difficult place. Because of human sin, the areas of human existence are very seldom simple and straightforward even in chronological sequence. His basic purpose was not to depict a chronological sequence but rather to depict how sin was judged and how God reigned and executed judgment not simply at the *end* of a process but while it was going on and forever! The cycles so far depicted attest to that conviction.

In the previous cycle of the seven seals, the basic religious teaching was that evil is self-destructive; in this cycle, that of the trumpets, it is clear that God actively takes part in the judgment process. These two ideas should be interpreted not as chronological sequences within history, one following the other, but rather as two processes which are ongoing at all times within the historical continuum. And each has its own "end"—the judgment on evil wherever and in whatever form it appears.

Questions for Further Consideration

1. List ways in which God's judgment falls directly on human sin.

2. How could the author of Revelation say in the midst of his work, when sin still seemed to be loose in the world, that "the kingdom of this world has become the kingdom of our Lord and of his Christ . . ."?

3. How does 10:8-11 relate to the witness of the church today toward present evils of our society? Be as specific as you can in applying this principle.

6. Chapters 12-14—Historical Summary

These chapters—typical of apocalyptic literature—give an historical survey explaining in weird symbolism just how the current situation came to be. The author was not able to depict a long, involved
process transpiring over several centuries since he was not writing
under a pseudonym as were many other apocayptic writers. Rather,
he concentrated on a more elaborately detailed account of the age in
which he lived. These chapters were John's historical summary.

12:1-6: And a great portent appeared in heaven, a woman clothed
with the sun, with the moon under her feet, and on her head a
crown of twelve stars; she was with child and she cried out in her
pangs of birth, in anguish for delivery. And another portent
appeared in heaven; behold, a great red dragon, with seven heads
and ten horns, and seven diadems upon his heads. His tail swept
down a third of the stars of heaven, and cast them to the earth. And
the dragon stood before the woman who was about to bear a child,
that he might devour her child when she brought it forth; she
brought forth a male child, one who is to rule all the nations with a
rod of iron, but her child was caught up to God and to his throne,
and the woman fled into the wilderness, where she has a place
prepared by God, in which to be nourished for one thousand two
hundred and sixty days.

A marvelous sign appeared in the sky. The woman symbolized the
people of God (note the crown with the *twelve* stars) from whom was
born the Messiah. But evil could not stand back and allow God's
agent of redemption to perform his work unchallenged. Therefore
Satan himself attempted to devour the child (perhaps a reference to
the crucifixion), but the child was taken up to God (the resurrection?). In the meantime, the woman fled to the wilderness, symbolic
of either safety or destruction. In this instance it was clearly the
former. And the time? Twelve hundred and sixty days or 3½ years!

Verses 7-12: Now war arose in heaven, Michael and his angels
fighting against the dragon; and the dragon and his angels fought,
but they were defeated and there was no longer any place for them
in heaven. And the great dragon was thrown down, that ancient
serpent, who is called the Devil and Satan, the deceiver of the
whole world—he was thrown down to the earth, and his angels
were thrown down with him. And I heard a loud voice in heaven,
saying, "Now the salvation and the power and the kingdom of our

God and the authority of his Christ have come, for the accuser of
our brethren has been thrown down, who accuses them day and
night before our God. And they have conquered him by the blood
of the Lamb and by the word of their testimony, for they loved not
their lives even unto death. Rejoice then, O heaven and you that
dwell therein! But woe to you, O earth and sea, for the devil has
come down to you in great wrath, because he knows that his time is
short!"

Michael, the patron angel of the people of God, was at this point
seen leading the cosmic battle against the forces of evil. Satan was
defeated, but his power was not yet destroyed. The struggles just
before death are often the most contested and so it is with evil. The
last moments of the Devil were to be spent on earth persecuting God's
people who continued to defeat him by their witness even to death.

Verses 13-17: And when the dragon saw that he had been thrown
down to the earth, he pursued the woman who had borne the male
child. But the woman was given the two wings of the great eagle
that she might fly from the serpent into the wilderness, to the place
where she is to be nourished for a time, and times, and half a time.
The serpent poured water like a river out of his mouth after the
woman, to sweep her away with the flood. But the earth came to the
help of the woman, and the earth opened its mouth and swallowed
the river which the dragon had poured from his mouth. Then the
dragon was angry with the woman, and went off to make war on
the rest of her offspring, on those who keep the commandments of
God and bear testimony to Jesus. And he stood on the sand of the
sea.

In a sense these verses simply reiterate what was said in verses 7-12.
The dragon made war on the woman (the people of God), but God
himself protected her in the times of crisis which lasted for the usual
$3\frac{1}{2}$ -year period of time.
The persons who were reading and hearing these words knew they
were living in this time of persecution. They were the ones with whom
the dragon was fighting. Exactly how the dragon pursued his
treachery was made known, again symbolically.

13:1-4: And I saw a beast rising out of the sea, with ten horns and
seven heads, with ten diadems upon its horns and a blasphemous
name upon its heads. And the beast that I saw was like a leopard, its

feet were like a bear's, and its mouth was like a lion's mouth. And to it the dragon gave his power and his throne and great authority. One of its heads seemed to have a mortal wound, but its mortal wound was healed, and the whole earth followed the beast with wonder. Men worshiped the dragon, for he had given his authority to the beast, and they worshiped the beast, saying, "Who is like the beast, and who can fight against it?"

The dragon summoned assistance in the form of a hideous monster which arose from the sea, the traditional source of evil and chaos. The beast is a composite of the four beasts of Daniel 7. The most important and curious aspect of this beast is that one of its heads had a mortal wound which had healed. (We shall say more about this shortly.) The important aspect to the writer of Revelation was the method by which Satan deceived humanity into worshiping him. He delegated his authority and power to the beast which was then worshiped by the people. They were worshiping Satan but not directly. It is simply not true that people will "sell their souls" to the Devil and directly worship him. Perhaps there are a few like Faust who would, but most persons refuse to do this. They will, however, fall prey to a clever disguise and worship evil in spite of themselves. This is the way in which evil usually operates, by deception.

Verses 5-10: And the beast was given a mouth uttering haughty and blasphemous words, and it was allowed to exercise authority for forty-two months; it opened its mouth to utter blasphemies against God, blaspheming his name and his dwelling, that is, those who dwell in heaven. Also it was allowed to make war on the saints and to conquer them. And authority was given it over every tribe and people and tongue and nation, and all who dwell on earth will worship it, every one whose name has not been written before the foundation of the world in the book of life of the Lamb that was slain. If any one has an ear, let him hear:
>If any one is to be taken captive,
>   to captivity he goes;
>if any one slays with the sword,
>   with the sword must he be slain.
Here is a call for the endurance and faith of the saints.

The beast, obviously symbolizing Rome and its might, was allowed to persecute the saints of God for forty-two months. John knew that most people would worship the beast. For those who remained faithful to God, however, there was to be a greater reward than any suffering they might have had to endure. It was at this point that John made mention of the "book of life of the Lamb" which had written within it the names of those who belonged to the people of God. Many persons misunderstand this figure; having one's name written in the book does not assure that person of a place among God's elect. Rather, it places a great burden on the person to remain faithful and loyal to God and Christ. There is assurance here, however, because the clear teaching is that once one's name is written in the book, no person or power can take it out—except one. The removal is ultimately in the hands of the person; only a person can take his or her name out of the book, and this occurs when the person betrays the faith that is beyond the powers of this world. "Here is a call for the endurance and faith of the saints" (verse 10b).

Verses 11-18: Then I saw another beast which rose out of the earth; it had two horns like a lamb and it spoke like a dragon. It exercises all the authority of the first beast in its presence, and makes the earth and its inhabitants worship the first beast, whose mortal wound was healed. It works great signs, even making fire come down from heaven to earth in the sight of men; and by the signs which it is allowed to work in the presence of the beast, it deceives those who dwell on earth, bidding them make an image for the beast which was wounded by the sword and yet lived; and it was allowed to give breath to the image of the beast so that the image of the beast should even speak, and to cause those who would not worship the image of the beast to be slain. Also it causes all, both small and great, both rich and poor, both free and slave, to be marked on the right hand or the forehead, so that no one can buy or sell unless he has the mark, that is, the name of the beast or the number of its name. This calls for wisdom: let him who has understanding reckon the number of the beast, for it is a human number, its number is six hundred and sixty-six.

There was at this point another beast, a parody of the Lamb, which arose from the earth. This probably indicates that it is a derivative of the other, the sea beast. It looked like a lamb but spoke like a dragon! From its description it becomes clear that this beast represents "false religion." It caused persons to worship the first beast and performed marvelous signs to awe people. We know from certain archaeological findings that priests had various ways of making idols or images talk, breathe fire and smoke, or perform other actions through the use of tubes, pulleys, and the like. In any case, it was another evidence of the deceit which evil and its emissaries resort to in their constant quest for the souls of human beings.

The false prophet, the second beast, had the authority to exercise almost complete control over the lives of persons. Those who did not conform to the wishes and desires of the dragon and its allies were marked with a sign so that even the necessities of life were denied to them. It is at this point that John introduced the curious and highly debated number, 666.

The reader is told that this is the name of the beast or the number of its name. In ancient times the alphabet was used for counting (as with Roman numerals); it was not until much later that the marvelous system of numerals came to the Western world through the Arabs. We are told in verse 18 that the number of the beast was a man's name. That it was a common practice to identify persons in those days by the sum total of the numerical values of their names is seen in wall inscriptions, one in particular where a person had written, "I love her whose number is 545."[1] To arrive at the number of a name, one simply adds together the numerical values of the letters of the name. Everyone, therefore, had a number. Exactly who this person was whose number was 666 has puzzled scholars and interpreters for many years. Various attempts have been made to figure out names in Greek or Latin which will total 666. No satisfactory solution has been found. Others have argued that since six is one short of seven, the perfect number, that it must represent evil; coming so close to perfection but falling short is one of the greatest sins one can imagine. This may be true, but there seems to be no evidence for such a theory. In no other apocalyptic work does six seem to symbolize evil; the plain indication of the text here is that the number was a *man's name*. There is one additional problem: in a number of Greek manuscripts the number is not 666 but 616. Any solution to the problem must take account of these factors.

No matter which solution a scholar espouses, it will not answer all the questions. There is a solution, however, which is supported by a large number of reputable scholars. This theory postulates that the name must be in Hebrew or Aramaic characters since so much of the background of Revelation seems to come from Semitic sources, and that if one spells *Neron Caesar* in Aramaic letters, the numerical equivalents of the letters total 666. It is also true that the last N on *Neron* is not necessary, and if it is omitted, the total is 616.

[1]G. A. Deissmann, *Light from the Ancient East,* trans. Lionel R. M. Strachan, rev. ed. (New York: George H. Doran Company, 1927), p. 277.

Further, if Nero was the one identified here, this would help to explain the meaning of the sea beast with seven heads, one of which had a mortal wound which had healed. Nero attempted to place the blame for the fire in Rome in the early sixties on the Christians and organized the first systematic persecution of the Christians by the Roman government. As far as we know, the persecution was limited to Rome. Because of the persecution and the character of the one who perpetuated these atrocities, however, Nero could become a symbol of the evil embodied in such an activity. Nero was supposed to have committed suicide by cutting his throat, but rumors persisted that he either was not dead or that he would rise from the dead to lead the Parthians against Rome. If this were to happen, it would be quite probable that he would lead an even greater persecution of the people of God. The evil and atrocities of Nero were part and parcel of the Roman state, a system centered on the emperor. These atrocities were directed by Rome on any who refused to worship the empire or its "divine" leaders. This enemy of God's people was no insignificant one but rather the most powerful and potentially demonic institution in the entire world. All the evil of the empire in general and Nero in particular is symbolized by the number of the beast, 666.

This passage is one of the most misunderstood in the entire book of Revelation. Many have attempted to read into the passage a prediction of some person or institution in the future who would appear at the "end of time." Through the centuries there have been numerous attempts to identify the beast and the person whose number is 666 and also to specify the mark of the beast. It would take too long to enumerate these fanciful guesses. Suffice it to say here that the beast was never intended to be a prediction of anything in the future—especially not the European common market—and the mark of the beast was not a prediction of the markings on packages that have begun to be used of late! These are two of the more recent "interpretations."

As we have seen from studying the passage, this is not a prediction of something or someone to come but a symbolic account of someone or something present *at the time of the original writing*. This description of the beast and the accompanying figures is part of the historical summary and should be interpreted as such.

14:1-5: Then I looked, and lo, on Mount Zion stood the Lamb, and with him a hundred and forty-four thousand who had his name and his Father's name written on their foreheads. And I heard a voice from heaven like the sound of many waters and like the sound of loud thunder; the voice I heard was like the sound of harpers playing on their harps, and they sing a new song before the throne and before the four living creatures and before the elders. No one could learn that song except the hundred and forty-four thousand who had been redeemed from the earth. It is these who have not defiled themselves with women, for they are chaste; it is these who follow the Lamb wherever he goes; these have been redeemed from mankind as first fruits for God and the Lamb, and in their mouth no lie was found, for they are spotless.

The historical survey continues. John saw the 144,000 who had God's name on their foreheads (see chapter 7:1-8); those who had been sealed would continue to reside with the Lamb. We learn that these were the ones who had not committed acts of blasphemy by idolatrous worship. This is the meaning of the curious statement about being "virgins." Unfaithfulness was a common symbolic designation of apostasy both in the Old Testament and in the New. These persons were "first fruits," that is, they were especially set apart for God's service, and they were blameless in word and deed.

Verses 6-11: Then I saw another angel flying in midheaven, with an eternal gospel to proclaim to those who dwell on earth, to every nation and tribe and tongue and people; and he said with a loud voice, "Fear God and give him glory, for the hour of his judgment has come; and worship him who made heaven and earth, and sea and the fountains of water."

Another angel, a second, followed, saying, "Fallen, fallen is Babylon the great, she who made all nations drink the wine of her impure passion."

And another angel, a third, followed them, saying with a loud voice, "If any one worships the beast and its image, and receives a mark on his forehead or on his hand, he also shall drink the wine of God's wrath, poured unmixed into the cup of his anger, and he shall be tormented with fire and sulphur in the presence of the holy angels and in the presence of the Lamb. And the smoke of their torment goes up for ever and ever; and they have no rest, day or night, these worshipers of the beast and its image, and whoever receives the mark of its name."

At this point three angels appeared. The first announced the gospel to the world—there was still time to repent, but the time was growing short. The second announced the sure fall of Babylon the great, a favorite designation of John for Rome. The third delivered a final ultimatum for those who persisted in their wickedness and who worshiped the beast. Their judgment was sure, and their judgment was deserved.

Verses 12-13: Here is a call for the endurance of the saints, those who keep the commandments of God and the faith of Jesus.

And I heard a voice from heaven saying, "Write this: Blessed are the dead who die in the Lord henceforth." "Blessed indeed," says the Spirit, "that they may rest from their labors, for their deeds follow them!"

Too often these verses are not understood properly because many commentators take this chapter as a prediction of the future judgment. In reality this chapter is, as we have indicated, a continuation of the historical survey which describes the situation of the church and its members at that moment. Understood against this background these verses become another call for remaining faithful in the face of terrible persecution. "Blessed are those who die in the Lord henceforth" (verse 13*b*) is a fairly plain statement that the situation for the people of God was to become increasingly more difficult and dangerous. They were assured, however, that their good deeds (not specific acts but loyalty to God) could not be taken away from them no matter how severe the persecution.

Verses 14-20: Then I looked, and lo, a white cloud, and seated on the cloud one like a son of man, with a golden crown on his head, and a sharp sickle in his hand. And another angel came out of the temple, calling with a loud voice to him who sat upon the cloud, "Put in your sickle, and reap, for the hour to reap has come, for the harvest of the earth is fully ripe." So he who sat upon the cloud swung his sickle on the earth, and the earth was reaped.

And another angel came out of the temple in heaven, and he too had a sharp sickle. Then another angel came out from the altar, the angel who has power over fire, and he called with a loud voice to him who had the sharp sickle, "Put in your sickle, and gather the clusters of the vine of the earth, for its grapes are ripe." So the angel swung his sickle on the earth and gathered the vintage of the earth, and threw it into the great wine press of the wrath of God; and the wine press was trodden outside the city and blood flowed from the wine press, as high as a horse's bridle, for one thousand six hundred stadia.

There is divided opinion among commentators about these verses. Some argue that these scenes depict a final judgment on the wicked; others argue that they are a warning to the faithful that more intense suffering was to come upon them. The latter commentators have the context to support their claim, but it seems to be clear that the scenes symbolize God's judgment on the earth. Actually both elements are probably included in these events.

John seems to have been arguing again in typical apocalyptic fashion that there would come a time when God intervened to judge the evil age; he would not stay his hand forever! Further, it was also true that when the judgment came, the people of God could be caught in it either by not getting away in time or by having the hatred of the oppressors more strongly directed at them because the oppressors saw the handwriting on the wall. Typically, in apocalyptic writings the last days of the reign of evil were the worst. During these times the forces of evil inflicted the worst possible hurt on the people of God. (For a similar idea, read 1 Corinthians 7:25-31.)

The figure of 1,600 stadia probably symbolizes the author's belief that the judgment would be for the entire earth. Since 1,600 is a combination of 4^2 (the number dealing with the created order) times 10^2 (the complete number), the 1,600 stadia probably are meant to symbolize the entire earth, not simply 184 miles—the result of translating the 1,600 stadia into specific distance.

How could the continued death of the people of God at the hands of the godless be a part of the ingathering in the time of judgment? It is curious indeed, but in all probability John saw the death of the martyrs as part of the judgment and part of the plan whereby the church witnessed to the world. Throughout this chapter the emphasis has been upon the death of God's elect, but it is a death which has meaning and consequences for the world and for the individual martyrs beyond the fact of mere physical death.

Questions for Further Consideration

1. List as many ways as you can in which evil attempts to obtain loyalty from human beings by means of deception and trickery.

2. How does one answer those who attempt to find in 666 a prediction of some great evil figure of the future? It is interesting that many persons and/or institutions have been suggested through the eras of church history as the fulfillment of this number, such as Martin Luther, the pope, the Roman Catholic Church, the Protestant churches, the Kaiser, Hitler, Tojo, Mussolini, and of late, the European common market, to name just a few!

3. How does suffering for one's faith affect others? Name some specific instances where such action was either successful or unsuccessful.

7. Chapters 15–16—Cycle of Judgment: The Seven Bowls of the Wrath of God

15:1-8: Then I saw another portent in heaven, great and wonderful, seven angels with seven plagues, which are the last, for with them the wrath of God is ended.

And I saw what appeared to be a sea of glass mingled with fire, and those who had conquered the beast and its image and the number of its name, standing beside the sea of glass with harps of God in their hands. And they sing the song of Moses, the servant of God, and the song of the Lamb, saying,

> "Great and wonderful are thy deeds,
> O Lord God the Almighty!
> Just and true are thy ways,
> O King of the ages!
> Who shall not fear and glorify thy
>   name, O Lord?
> For thou alone art holy.
> All nations shall come and worship
>   thee,
> for thy judgments have been
>   revealed."

After this I looked, and the temple of the tent of witness in heaven was opened, and out of the temple came the seven angels with the seven plagues, robed in pure bright linen, and their breasts girded with golden girdles. And one of the four living creatures gave the seven angels seven golden bowls full of the wrath of God who lives for ever and ever; and the temple was filled with smoke from the glory of God and from his power, and no one could enter the temple until the seven plagues of the seven angels were ended.

John came finally to the last cycle of judgment. The hand of God had been held back in the hope that some others might turn and join the people of God. God in his infinite mercy had delayed the conclusive judgment so that everyone would have the opportunity to repent. But there comes a point at which God's justice overtakes his mercy; in the book of Revelation that time had come.

The fact that this was the *last* cycle of judgment did not necessarily mean that this was the *last* judgment on all the world. It seems to mean, however, in the context of this book as a whole, the last judgment as far as the persecutors of God's people were concerned. There does come a time when partial judgment must give way to final judgment, but this was final judgment on a particular person, group of persons, or institution. In other words, there are many "final" judgments going on in human history at *all* times. There comes a time when God's mercy ceases to predominate, and his justice is exercised.

These two chapters are filled with Old Testament symbols and allusions, especially those connected with the Exodus event. The sea of glass was mingled with fire, a symbol of God's judgment, and surrounding the sea were the martyrs singing the Song of Moses and the Lamb (perhaps a song of deliverance). At this point the seven angels were given seven bowls of the wrath of God.

16:1-9: Then I heard a loud voice from the temple telling the seven angels, "Go and pour out on the earth the seven bowls of the wrath of God."

So the first angel went and poured his bowl on the earth, and foul and evil sores came upon the men who bore the mark of the beast and worshiped its image.

The second angel poured his bowl into the sea, and it became like the blood of a dead man, and every living thing died that was in the sea.

The third angel poured his bowl into the rivers and the fountains of water, and they became blood. And I heard the angel of water say,

> "Just art thou in these thy
>   judgments,
> thou who art and wast, O Holy One.
> For men have shed the blood of
>   saints and prophets,
> and thou hast given them blood to
>   drink.
> It is their due!"
> And I heard the altar cry,
>   "Yea, Lord God the Almighty,
>   true and just are thy judgments!"

The fourth angel poured his bowl on the sun, and it was allowed to scorch men with fire; men were scorched by the fierce heat, and they cursed the name of God who had power over these plagues, and they did not repent and give him glory.

The first four angels poured out their bowls of wrath on the earth, particularly upon those who had the mark of the beast. It was here that John used the Exodus symbolism to illustrate the biblical concept that the punishment should fit the crime. These people had been responsible for the death of the martyrs, shedding innocent blood; now they were forced to drink blood! Even with the fourth bowl God would have been willing to accept their repentance, but instead they cursed God and refused to honor him.

> Verses 10-16: The fifth angel poured his bowl on the throne of the beast, and its kingdom was in darkness; men gnawed their tongues in anguish and cursed the God of heaven for their pain and sores, and did not repent of their deeds. The sixth angel poured his bowl on the great river Euphrates, and its water was dried up, to prepare the way for the kings from the east. And I saw, issuing from the mouth of the dragon and from the mouth of the beast and from the mouth of the false prophet, three foul spirits like frogs; for they are demonic spirits, performing signs, who go abroad to the kings of the whole world, to assemble them for battle on the great day of God the Almighty. ("Lo, I am coming like a thief! Blessed is he who is awake, keeping his garments that he may not go naked and be seen exposed!") And they assembled them at the place which is called in Hebrew Armageddon.

With the last three bowls the wrath of God was directed primarily at the source of the evil persecution. The fifth bowl scored a direct hit on the very throne of the beast. The sixth prepared the way for an invasion upon Rome by the kings of the East. The place where these forces were to be gathered for battle was called "Armageddon." What person cannot recall the dreadful stories about this strange and mysterious place!

There are several aspects to remember about Armageddon, however. First, it is not the place of the final great battle which will conclude history; it is only the place where armies would be assembled anticipating a battle, the battle depicting a form of judgment on Rome. As with almost everything in Revelation, Armageddon is symbolic. It represents a decisive battle in the affairs of the people of God. The term "Armageddon" is from the Hebrew— the two words which together form the Greek term which means "Mount of Megiddo." In the Old Testament world Megiddo was the scene for several decisive battles because of its unique location near the Valley of Jezreel or Plain of Esdraelon. Invading armies had to enter the land from the north through this passageway. Its strategic location assured that many significant battles would be fought at Megiddo. Two are recounted in Judges 5 and 2 Kings 23:28-30. Solomon kept a large contingent of military personnel and equipment there during the great days of his kingship. Thus, it only seems fitting that one of the locations for the last seven bowls of God's wrath would be placed symbolically near Megiddo.

> Verses 17-21: The seventh angel poured his bowl into the air, and a great voice came out of the temple, from the throne, saying, "It is done!" And there were flashes of lightning, voices, peals of thunder, and a great earthquake such as had never been since men were on the earth, so great was that earthquake. The great city was split into three parts, and the cities of the nations fell, and God remembered great Babylon, to make her drain the cup of the fury of his wrath. And every island fled away, and no mountains were to be found; and great hailstones, heavy as a hundredweight, dropped on men from heaven, till men cursed God for the plague of the hail, so fearful was that plague.

The seventh angel poured his bowl into the air; and when this happened, mighty Babylon was split apart. There is no thought here about the end of time or history, but only about the judgment upon the power that was using its demonic might to thwart the purposes of God and to kill his people. Even here at the very end of the persecutor's power, people still refused to worship God and in fact cursed him because of the judgment! How typical of humankind!

Questions for Further Consideration

1. List examples from personal experience or from history in which evil has had ample opportunity to repent (but has instead refused) and has finally been destroyed. What does this teach us about the mercy of God and the justice of God?

2. Discuss or reflect upon the idea that there are many "final" judgments in human history and in human life individually. In what ways do these events affect the continuing flow of human history and life?

8. Chapters 17-20—The Judgment of the Harlot City and the End of the Persecution

Verses 1-6: Then one of the seven angels who had the seven bowls came and said to me, "Come, I will show you the judgment of the great harlot who is seated upon many waters, with whom the kings of the earth have committed fornication, and with the wine of whose fornication the dwellers on earth have become drunk." And he carried me away in the Spirit into a wilderness, and I saw a woman sitting on a scarlet beast which was full of blasphemous names, and it had seven heads and ten horns. The woman was arrayed in purple and scarlet, and bedecked with gold and jewels and pearls, holding in her hand a golden cup full of abominations and the impurities of her fornication; and on her forehead was written a name of mystery: "Babylon the great, mother of harlots and of earth's abominations." And I saw the woman, drunk with the blood of the saints and the blood of the martyrs of Jesus.

John gave a more detailed account of the fall of Rome. Told in rich and sometimes confusing (to us) symbolism, the scene he depicted was indeed awesome. John was taken again to the wilderness, a safe place, to view the judgment of the great harlot, the one who had seduced the people of the world into blasphemous and immoral lives. She was seated on a scarlet beast, bedecked in royal finery, holding in her hand a gold, jeweled cup full of the impurities of her fornication. The author again showed the deceptive power of evil and by this very graphic and sickening figure indicated just what the inner content of such a life was. The woman had a name, Babylon, and she was drunk with the blood of the martyrs of Jesus.

We know that this woman represents Rome. (See 1 Peter 5:13 for another New Testament example where Rome is called Babylon.)

Verses 7-14: When I saw her I marveled greatly. But the angel said to me, "Why marvel? I will tell you the mystery of the woman, and of the beast with seven heads and ten horns that carries her. The beast that you saw was, and is not, and is to ascend from the bottomless pit and go to perdition; and the dwellers on earth whose names have not been written in the book of life from the foundation of the world, will marvel to behold the beast, because it was and is not and is to come. This calls for a mind with wisdom: the seven heads are seven mountains on which the woman is seated; they are also seven kings, five of whom have fallen, one is, the other has not yet come, and when he comes he must remain only a little while. As for the beast that was and is not, it is an eighth but it belongs to the seven, and it goes to perdition. And the ten horns that you saw are ten kings who have not yet received royal power, but they are to receive authority as kings for one hour, together with the beast. These are of one mind and give over their power and authority to the beast; they will make war on the Lamb, and the Lamb will conquer them, for he is Lord of lords and Kings of kings, and those with him are called and chosen and faithful."

In order to dispel doubt, the author sought to explain the vision. The beast upon which the woman was seated was the beast which appeared in the beginning of the thirteenth chapter. This creature is also a parody of truth since it "was and is not and is to come." Here we probably have again a reference to the idea that Nero (or one like him) would return to make war on God's people. It does not appear that John was so much interested in Nero actually rising from the dead as he was in pointing out that evil is continually reborn and continually grows. But the great truth which God's people know is that this beast arose from the jaws of hell and was destined to return to the jaws of hell!

The reader is then told that the seven heads (of the monster) represent seven hills on which the woman was seated. For centuries Rome had been known as the city built on seven hills. Can there be any doubt that this is what is meant here? But the author of Revelation, as we have seen on several occasions, could use his symbols in more than one way and with more than one meaning. The seven heads also represented the emperors of Rome. Many commentators have become frustrated attempting to determine which emperors were intended. The fact that there are seven should be the clue to any reader that the important point is the idea of a completed number rather than individual identities. We are told that five had died, one was, and another would come but remain only a "little while." The intent of this is again to encourage hope and endurance in the people of God who were undergoing persecution. The fact that they were in the time of the sixth ruler and that the seventh would rule only a short period means to the people that while the end was not to come immediately, it would indeed be soon. So the message is "hold fast to the faith." Evil would intensify, but its time was very short. The beast was an eighth but belonged to the seven; this curious description probably means that the seven emperors (symbolic of the total number of rulers) derived their power and demonic hatred from the beast as they in turn by their use of that

power caused the beast to live and grow. But John's point is clear;
they all went to hell!

Now John turned to the ten horns on the beast. These represent ten
kings, probably vassal kings under Roman control in the provinces,
and they assisted the beast in making war on the Lamb.

> Verses 15-18: And he said to me, "The waters that you saw, where
> the harlot is seated, are peoples and multitudes and nations and
> tongues. And the ten horns that you saw, they and the beast will
> hate the harlot; they will make her desolate and naked, and devour
> her flesh and burn her up with fire, for God has put it into their
> hearts to carry out his purpose by being of one mind and giving
> over their royal power to the beast, until the words of God shall be
> fulfilled. And the woman that you saw is the great city which has
> dominion over the kings of the earth."

The interpreter further explained to John certain aspects of the
vision. The waters represent the entire earth over which the harlot
had control. But oddly enough, John learned, there was no "honor
among thieves," except for self-preservation. Evil turned upon itself,
for the ten vassal kings and the beast turned upon the harlot and
destroyed her. Evil is self-destructive and, like a fire, consumes itself.

The reader is then left with no possible way to miss the meaning. In
verse 18 the author clearly says, "And the woman you saw is the great
city which has dominion over the kings of the earth." If this is not
Rome, what else could it be?

> 18:1-8: After this I saw another angel coming down from heaven,
> having great authority; and the earth was made bright with his
> splendor. And he called out with a mighty voice,
>> "Fallen, fallen is Babylon the great!
>> It has become a dwelling place of
>> demons,
>> a haunt of every foul spirit,
>> a haunt of every foul and hateful bird;
>> for all nations have drunk the wine
>> of her impure passion,
>> and the kings of the earth have
>> committed fornication with her,
>> and the merchants of the earth have
>> grown rich with the wealth of
>> her wantonness."

Then I heard another voice from heaven saying,
"Come out of her, my people,
lest you take part in her sins,
lest you share in her plagues;
for her sins are heaped high as
heaven,
and God has remembered her
iniquities.
Render to her as she herself has
rendered,
and repay her double for her deeds;
mix a double draught for her in the
cup she mixed.
As she glorified herself and played
the wanton,
so give her a like measure of torment
and mourning.
Since in her heart she says, 'A queen
I sit,
I am no widow, mourning I shall
never see,'
So shall her plagues come in a single
day,
pestilence and mourning and famine,
and she shall be burned with fire;
for mighty is the Lord God who
judges her."

Another angel proclaimed a funeral dirge over the harlot city. There are two Old Testament passages (Jeremiah 50–51 and Ezekiel 26–27) which were probably utilized by the author of Revelation as models for this particular poem of judgment. These verses, however, are even more magnificent in their depiction of God's vengeance on the evil persecutor of his people. Too often readers of the book of Revelation are appalled at what they see as a vindictive approach to judgment. This is easy to understand, but finding only vengeance here means that the reader has missed the point that the author was attempting to make. For example, the first thing that should strike a reader about these verses is the note of tragedy in them. Here was the greatest civilization that that part of the.world had ever known—a civilization with potential for all kinds of good—but evil, greed, corruption, and hatred came to dominate that great city so much so that its sins, when heaped together, reached to heaven itself! In such a situation justice had to be rendered; God's laws were to be obeyed, not Rome's, and when any civilization or institution (even the church) is in conflict with God's will and purpose, it stands under God's judgment.

In verse 4 there is a summons, again typical of apocalyptic writing, for the people of God to come out of this society. The people of God should have been wise enough to read the signs of the times and to get away from the sure judgment that would fall on the wicked city (see Mark 13:14-27).

Verses 9-19: And the kings of the earth, who committed fornication and were wanton with her, will weep and wail over her when they see the smoke of her burning; they will stand far off, in fear of her torment, and say,
> "Alas! alas! thou great city,
> thou mighty city, Babylon!
> In one hour has thy judgment come."

And the merchants of the earth weep and mourn for her, since no one buys their cargo any more, cargo of gold, silver, jewels and pearls, fine linen, purple, silk and scarlet, all kinds of scented wood, all articles of ivory, all articles of costly wood, bronze, iron and marble, cinnamon, spice, incense, myrrh, frankincense, wine, oil, fine flour and wheat, cattle and sheep, horses and chariots, and slaves, that is, human souls.
> "The fruit for which thy soul longed
> has gone from thee,
> and all thy dainties and thy splendor
> are lost to thee, never to be
> found again!"

The merchants of these wares, who gained wealth from her, will stand far off, in fear of her torment, weeping and mourning aloud,
> "Alas, alas, for the great city
> that was clothed in fine linen, in
> purple and scarlet,
> bedecked with gold, with jewels, and
> with pearls!
> In one hour all this wealth has been
> laid waste."

And all shipmasters and seafaring men, sailors and all whose trade is on the sea, stood far off and cried out as they saw the smoke of her burning,

"What city was like the great city?"
And they threw dust on their heads, as they wept and mourned, crying out,

> "Alas, alas, for the great city
> where all who had ships at sea
> grew rich by her wealth!
> In one hour she has been laid waste."

The scene shifts to those who had allied themselves with the great harlot, the wicked city Babylon, for their own gain. The kings, merchants, shipmasters, and sailors all profited from their relationship with Rome. They cared not for her but only for themselves. They stood "afar off." While they were not directly affected by her judgment, they were indirectly affected since their source of livelihood had been destroyed. Again there is the tremendous note of tragedy since all the potential for good in Rome's greatness had been prostituted on the altar of human greed allied with demonic evil. There is nothing wrong with trade and commerce in themselves, but when profit and gain are placed first, to be pursued at all costs, and when such trade reaches out to include a traffic in human lives, then that system stands condemned before the majesty and righteousness of almighty God!

Verses 20-24:

> "Rejoice over her, O heaven,
> O saints and apostles and prophets,
> for God has given judgment for you
> against her!"

Then a mighty angel took up a stone like a great millstone and threw it into the sea, saying,

> "So shall Babylon the great city be
> thrown down with violence,
> and shall be found no more;
> and the sound of harpers and
> minstrels, of flute players and
> trumpeters,
> shall be heard in thee no more;
> and a craftsmen of any craft
> shall be found in thee no more;
> and the sound of the millstone
> shall be heard in thee no more;
> and the light of a lamp

> shall shine in thee no more;
> and the voice of bridegroom and
>   bride
> shall be heard in thee no more;
> for thy merchants were the great
>   men of the earth,
> and all nations were deceived by
>   thy sorcery.
> And in her was found the blood of
>   prophets and of saints,
> and of all who have been slain on
>   earth."

There follows a sign, like the prophetic signs of the Old Testament, depicting Babylon as a millstone cast into the sea to illustrate the judgment that would come upon her. Her dwelling place would indeed be desolate.

19:1-5: After this I heard what seemed to be the mighty voice of a great multitude in heaven, crying,

> "Hallelujah! Salvation and glory and
>   power belong to our God,
> for his judgments are true and just;
> he has judged the great harlot who
>   corrupted the earth with her
>   fornication,
> and he has avenged on her the blood
>   of his servants."

Once more they cried,

> "Hallelujah! The smoke from her
>   goes up for ever and ever."

And the twenty-four elders and the four living creatures fell down and worshiped God who is seated on the throne, saying, "Amen. Hallelujah!" And from the throne came a voice crying, "Praise our God, all you his servants, you who fear him, small and great."

Then the scene shifts to heaven where the host around the throne of God praised him for his justice and majesty. He acted in accordance with his nature!

19:6-10: Then I heard what seemed to be the voice of a great multitude, like the sound of many waters and like the sound of mighty thunderpeals, crying,

> "Hallelujah! For the Lord our God
> the Almighty reigns.
> Let us rejoice and exult and give
> him the glory,
> for the marriage of the Lamb has
> come,
> and his Bride has made herself
> ready;
> it was granted her to be clothed with
> fine linen, bright and pure"—

for the fine linen is the righteous deeds of the saints.

And the angel said to me, "Write this: Blessed are those who are invited to the marriage supper of the Lamb." And he said to me, "These are true words of God." Then I fell down at his feet to worship him, but he said to me, "You must not do that! I am a fellow servant with you and your brethren who hold the testimony of Jesus. Worship God." For the testimony of Jesus is the spirit of prophecy.

The announcement is made of the marriage of the Lamb to the church, represented by the faithful who had not defiled themselves with the image and morality of the beast. Further, there was to be a marriage feast, a symbol of God's presence with his people in the new age. John was so awed with all these events and visions and revelations that he fell down to worship the angel. But he was sharply reprimanded and told explicitly that only God was to be worshiped. This was a clear reminder to the church that not even an angel, much less an emperor, was due homage; this worship was reserved for God alone.

Verses 11-16: Then I saw heaven opened, and behold, a white horse! He who sat upon it is called Faithful and True, and in righteousness he judges and makes war. His eyes are like a flame of fire, and on his head are many diadems; and he has a name inscribed which no one knows but himself. He is clad in a robe dipped in blood, and the name by which he is called is The Word of God. And the armies of heaven, arrayed in fine linen, white and pure, followed him on white horses. From his mouth issues a sharp sword with which to smite the nations, and he will rule them with a rod of iron; he will tread the wine press of the fury of the wrath of God the Almighty. On his robe and on his thigh he has a name inscribed, King of kings and Lord of lords.

Another rider on a white horse appeared. This was not the same horseman as that in 6:1; the only similarity is in the fact that both rode white horses, symbolic of victory. This rider was called Faithful and True, and his robe had been dipped in blood. Again commentators do not agree—here, about the source of the blood. Was this the blood of his enemies? Or was it that of his followers who had been martyred for their witness? Was it his own blood shed on the cross? In all probability there is some truth in each of these theories. In any event the rider is the Word of God, and he was followed by armies of his victorious faithful ones riding white horses. The reader is told clearly in verse 15 that the rider's presence here was for the purpose of judgment, for the three figures given in this verse all point to the execution of justice. The rider could exercise this function because he had earned the right to be called King of kings and Lord of lords!

Verses 17-21: Then I saw an angel standing in the sun, and with a loud voice he called to all the birds that fly in mid-heaven, "Come, gather for the great supper of God, to eat the flesh of kings, the flesh of captains, the flesh of mighty men, the flesh of horses and their riders, and the flesh of all men, both free and slave, both small and great." And I saw the beast and the kings of the earth with their armies gathered to make war against him who sits upon the horse and against his army. And the beast was captured, and with it the false prophet who in its presence had worked the signs by which he deceived those who had received the mark of the beast and those who worshiped its image. These two were thrown alive into the lake of fire that burns with sulphur. And the rest were slain by the sword of him who sits upon the horse, the sword that issues from his mouth; and all the birds were gorged with their flesh.

In this section the defeat of the beast and the false prophet along with their followers is described. The birds of the air were summoned to "clean up" the human debris after the battle. The beast and false prophet, however, were thrown into the lake of fire. The reader is not told at this point exactly what this is. That the fire is a symbol of God's judgment is clear enough for the present.

20:1-6: Then I saw an angel coming down from heaven, holding in his hand the key of the bottomless pit and a great chain. And he seized the dragon, that ancient serpent, who is the Devil and Satan, and bound him for a thousand years, and threw him into the pit, and shut it and sealed it over him, that he should deceive the nations no more, till the thousand years were ended. After that he must be loosed for a little while.

Then I saw thrones, and seated on them were those to whom judgment was committed. Also I saw the souls of those who had been beheaded for their testimony to Jesus and for the word of God, and who had not worshiped the beast or its image and had not received its mark on their foreheads or their hands. They came to life, and reigned with Christ a thousand years. The rest of the dead did not come to life until the thousand years were ended. This is the first resurrection. Blessed and holy is he who shares in the first resurrection! Over such the second death has no power, but they shall be priests of God and of Christ, and they shall reign with him a thousand years.

These verses are among the most misunderstood of any scriptural passage. For some unknown reason, upon coming to these verses even those persons who interpret the book of Revelation as a writing full of symbolism and imagery feel that these verses should be taken in some kind of literal sense rather than the usual symbolic sense in which they have taken almost everything else in the book, especially the numbers!

The point of these verses seems to be a symbolic representation of the special reward which the martyrs would receive. There is nothing here about a rule on earth, nor about the advent of Christ, but only that the martyrs would reign completely with Christ because of their witness to their faith. There is in some apocalyptic works a theory about a period of time between the persecution and the final battle with evil, and this idea is surely reflected here. But John was never bound by tradition; he always used it to fit his own categories in order to tell his own story.

The one thousand-year binding of Satan is, then, a symbolic way of saying that Satan was completely bound. And he is completely bound where men and women give their witness to God and his Christ totally and completely. For those who did make such a witness in John's time and were killed for their faith, there was a special reward. This special reward for the martyrs was John's way of encouraging faith and loyalty in the people to whom he was writing. It was also his way of saying that persons who are loyal to God will participate in the binding of Satan. The one who remains faithful to death will share in the joys of the first resurrection. Over these people the second death has no power. And as with the lake of fire, the second death is not yet defined.

Verses 7-10: And when the thousand years are ended, Satan will be loosed from his prison and will come out to deceive the nations which are at the four corners of the earth, that is, Gog and Magog, to gather them for battle; their number is like the sand of the sea. And they marched up over the broad earth and surrounded the camp of the saints and the beloved city; but fire came down from heaven and consumed them, and the devil who had deceived them was thrown into the lake of fire and sulphur where the beast and the false prophet were, and they will be tormented day and night for ever and ever.

That these verses were not intended to be interpreted as a chronological scheme is brought home clearly in the Greek text of verse 7 which says, "And *wherever* the thousand years may [should] be completed [brought to maturity, brought to a purposeful conclusion]. . . ." This indicates that John was not thinking in terms of chronology as much as he was in terms of status. The martyrs were bound to Christ completely—*there* Satan was bound. The nations were not bound to Christ—*there* Satan was free to deceive them.

All of the people who are deceived by Satan are enemies of God's people. The terms "Gog" and "Magog" are symbolic representations of the forces of evil and the enemies of God and his people. It is of great significance that John did not here depict a great battle with blood running up to the horses' bridles, but rather God himself disposes of the evil mass of people. And in typical apocalyptic fashion John showed that God is the one who is really in control, because at his wish, the devil is thrown into the lake of fire where his cohorts, the beast and false prophet, already are residing!

Verses 11-15: Then I saw a great white throne and him who sat upon it; from his presence earth and sky fled away, and no place was found for them. And I saw the dead, great and small, standing before the throne, and books were opened. Also another book was opened, which is the book of life. And the dead were judged by what was written in the books, by what they had done. And the sea gave up the dead in it, Death and Hades gave up the dead in them, and all were judged by what they had done. Then Death and Hades were thrown into the lake of fire. This is the second death, the lake of fire; and if any one's name was not found written in the book of life, he was thrown into the lake of fire.

To bolster his point, John depicted the scene of judgment where there was no room for any who held pretentious claims to power and authority. Only God reigns supreme over all. It is interesting also that even though salvation is always given through the commitment of the person to God, judgment nevertheless is upon one's works (see chapters 2–3). All persons stand under the ultimate judgment of God —make no mistake about that!

John reminded his readers again that real death is not physical death. In the view of both the Old and New Testaments physical death is never looked upon as a curse but rather as a natural part of the created order of God's universe. The tragedy of death is the tragedy of dying apart from God. Physical death itself, unless it comes too soon or in some tragic fashion, is not a tragedy. John made this point clearly here. It is not the first death, i.e., physical death, that people should fear, but rather, people should fear that worse death, the second death. The second death is a death of the spirit which is not in the proper relationship with God. This is the second death and the lake of fire—being separated from God! John's message is loud and clear—this life counts and counts heavily, for in it people make choices and commitments which have ultimate meaning and significance. ". . . if any one's name was not found written in the book of life, that person was thrown into the lake of fire" (verse 15). No one, no power, can take your name from that book except you yourself!

These verses are marvelous verses which deal with a person's ultimate destiny, but they are not a chronology of the end of time! They do indeed, however, deal with ultimate matters. One of the problems so many persons have with "eschatology" is that today we tend to think of that term solely in connection with the "ultimate end," chronologically speaking. The biblical writers, for the most part, viewed eschatology more as a teleology, i.e., a bringing to completion or maturity, the reaching of a goal. This may involve the "ultimate end" but it does not require such a concept. What the biblical writers emphasized was that "ultimate" events could happen within the historical spectrum. It was not so much with "postremity"—that is, events surrounding the ultimate end of time—that the writers were concerned as with a "finality" which did not necessarily imply "extremity"! This is the basic underlying idea taught in this passage. *Ultimate* decisions do not necessarily have to be *final* decisions. We are dealing here with ultimate commitment of one's life to God, commitment which can and should occur now, not at the end!

Questions for Further Consideration

1. Since Rome is identified as the Great Harlot in chapter 17, are there other nations or institutions in history that you can recall that "fit" that description? How?

2. Since the great sin of Rome's commercialism was dealing in human lives, can you think of ways that human lives are still "bartered" in our contemporary culture?

3. Many persons have interpreted chapter 20 and the "one thousand years" as a part of the "coming of Jesus." Does the text make this connection? Why do you think so many attempt to make of this passage a description of the "end of time"? Why is it illegitimate to do so?

9. Chapters 21:1-22:5—Vision of the Transformed Age

21:1-8: Then I saw a new heaven and a new earth; for the first heaven and the first earth had passed away, and the sea was no more. And I saw the holy city, new Jerusalem, coming down out of heaven from God, prepared as a bride adorned for her husband; and I heard a great voice from the throne saying, "Behold, the dwelling of God is with men. He will dwell with them, and they shall be his people, and God himself will be with them; he will wipe away every tear from their eyes, and death shall be no more, neither shall there be mourning nor crying nor pain any more, for the former things have passed away."

And he who sat upon the throne said, "Behold, I make all things new." Also he said, "Write this, for these words are trustworthy and true." And he said to me, "It is done! I am the Alpha and the Omega, the beginning and the end. To the thirsty I will give from the fountain of the water of life without payment. He who conquers shall have this heritage, and I will be his God and he shall be my son. But as for the cowardly, the faithless, the polluted, as for murderers, fornicators, sorcerers, idolaters, and all liars, their lot shall be in the lake that burns with fire and sulphur, which is the second death."

At this point John experienced a magnificent scene which depicted life as it would be when God truly lives with humankind. The scene is not a description of heaven, as many have supposed, but rather the picture of a transformed earth where the sea, that source of evil and chaos, was no more! It is clear that this new, transformed society could not be built by humankind, but would only come as a gift of God. To participate in this new life meant that all former things had passed away; a new set of standards and values would be observed. And anyone who wished to participate could do so. Such a commitment would not be easy since the person would have to face opposition of a severe and harsh kind; for the one who remained faithful to the very end, however, there would be the reward of God's presence. This new life was not for the cowardly since much courage was needed to keep one's faith untarnished by the world. The future of those who did not participate rested in the lake of fire, the second death, separation from God.

Verses 9-21: Then came one of the seven angels who had the seven bowls full of the seven last plagues, and spoke to me, saying, "Come, I will show you the Bride, the wife of the Lamb." And in the

Spirit he carried me away to a great, high mountain, and showed me the holy city Jerusalem coming down out of heaven from God, having the glory of God, its radiance like a most rare jewel, like a jasper, clear as crystal. It had a great, high wall, with twelve gates, and at the gates twelve angels, and on the gates the names of the twelve tribes of the sons of Israel were inscribed; on the east three gates, on the north three gates, on the south three gates, and on the west three gates. And the wall of the city had twelve foundations, and on them the twelve names of the twelve apostles of the Lamb.

And he who talked to me had a measuring rod of gold to measure the city and its gates and walls. The city lies foursquare, its length the same as its breadth; and he measured the city with his rod, twelve thousand stadia; its length and breadth and height are equal. He also measured its wall, a hundred and forty-four cubits by a man's measure, that is, an angel's. The wall was built of jasper, while the city was pure gold, clear as glass. The foundations of the wall of the city were adorned with every jewel; the first was jasper, the second sapphire, the third agate, the fourth emerald, the fifth onyx, the sixth carnelian, the seventh chrysolite, the eighth beryl, the ninth topaz, the tenth chrysoprase, the eleventh jacinth, the twelfth amethyst. And the twelve gates were twelve pearls, each of the gates made of a single pearl, and the street of the city was pure gold, transparent as glass.

At this point John gave his famous description of the new Jerusalem, a city of splendor, worthy to be the bride of the Lamb. The new Jerusalem was not stained as that other city, the harlot, a city drunk with the blood of the saints. The description of the new Jerusalem is magnificent, and the reader cannot miss the use of the number twelve throughout the description. It was the city of God's people depicted as a perfect cube, probably with reference to the Holy of Holies where God's Presence was especially felt and experienced. But in contrast to that place which could only be entered once a year by the High Priest, this city had God's Presence every day available for all the people!

21:22–22:5: And I saw no temple in the city, for its temple is the Lord God the Almighty and the Lamb. And the city has no need of sun or moon to shine upon it, for the glory of God is its light, and its lamp is the Lamb. By its light shall the nations walk; and the kings of the earth shall bring their glory into it, and its gates shall never be shut by day—and there shall be no night there; they shall bring into it the glory and the honor of the nations. But nothing unclean shall enter it, nor any one who practices abomination or falsehood, but only those who are written in the Lamb's book of life.

Then he showed me the river of the water of life, bright as crystal, flowing from the throne of God and of the Lamb through the middle of the street of the city; also, on either side of the river, the tree of life with its twelve kinds of fruit, yielding its fruit each month; and the leaves of the tree were for the healing of the nations. There shall no more be anything accursed, but the throne of God and of the Lamb shall be in it, and his servants shall worship him; they shall see his face, and his name shall be on their foreheads. And night shall be no more; they need no light of lamp or sun, for the Lord God will be their light, and they shall reign for ever and ever.

Because God was present so vividly there was no temple in this city; God was present and every act of each person was an act of worship. God is not limited by time or space or geographical locale; in this place his people would not be limited to where or how often they could worship him. He would be present always, and his people would worship him by every act of their lives!

One very interesting but often overlooked aspect of this portrait of "Paradise Regained" is John's realistic understanding that even in this new era, even with the new Jerusalem, there would yet be human freedom which can and would say "No" to God. This is not a picture of a city in heaven but a city on earth; in spite of the fact that the saints of God were experiencing great joys by having the persecution removed and God's presence to them even closer, there were still those who could and would refuse God's gifts. John never said that sin would be removed from the earth, only that the people of God, experiencing persecution now, would not be hurt by it any longer (verse 27).

John's vision includes the tree of life which was available to all, and whose leaves had a healing ingredient for the nations—if they would accept the medicine! What John was really stressing in his highly symbolic and majestic vision was that the people of God would have the persecution removed and would dwell secure again from the powers of evil in close relationship with God and witnessing to his gift of life.

10. Chapter 22:6-21—Epilogue

And he said to me, "These words are trustworthy and true. And the Lord, the God of the spirits of the prophets, has sent his angel to show his servants what must soon take place. And behold, I am coming soon."

Blessed is he who keeps the words of the prophecy of this book.

I John am he who heard and saw these things. And when I heard and saw them, I fell down to worship at the feet of the angel who showed them to me; but he said to me, "You must not do that! I am a fellow servant with you and your brethren the prophets, and with those who keep the words of this book. Worship God."

And he said to me, "Do not seal up the words of the prophecy of this book, for the time is near. Let the evildoer still do evil, and the filthy still be filthy, and the righteous still do right, and the holy still be holy."

"Behold, I am coming soon, bringing my recompense, to repay every one for what he has done. I am the Alpha and the Omega, the first and the last, the beginning and the end."

Blessed are those who wash their robes, that they may have the right to the tree of life and that they may enter the city by the gates. Outside are the dogs and sorcerers and fornicators and murderers and idolaters, and every one who loves and practices falsehood.

"I Jesus have sent my angel to you with this testimony for the churches. I am the root and the offspring of David, the bright morning star."

The Spirit and the Bride say, "Come." And let him who hears say, "Come." And let him who is thirsty come, let him who desires take the water of life without price.

I warn every one who hears the words of the prophecy of this book: if any one adds to them, God will add to him the plagues described in this book, and if any one takes away from the words of the book of this prophecy, God will take away his share in the tree of life and in the holy city, which are described in this book.

He who testifies to these things says, "Surely I am coming soon." Amen. Come, Lord Jesus!

The grace of the Lord Jesus be with all the saints. Amen.

Four times in these verses John reminded the readers and hearers that the time was "soon." In fact, verses 10-11 seem to imply that the time was so short that there was now almost no chance for change. He further enforced this notion by indicating that these words were *not* to be sealed up for a later time (as with most apocalyptic works) but were for the immediate future.

He reiterated that *no* creature was to be worshiped—God alone was to receive this honor. There was also a warning about anyone who may have been tempted to change any of the words of his prophecy; such an action would bring upon that person the judgment of God as described previously. There is then another assurance that the time is short, that Jesus would be coming in judgment soon; the book then concludes with a blessing for all the people of God.

Questions for Further Consideration

1. Many commentators have attempted to rearrange the text of Revelation in these chapters because evil appears to be still existent in spite of the seeming "finality" of God's judgment. How do you explain this against the backdrop of apocalyptic literature?

2. Examine the symbolism of the "New Jerusalem" very carefully. What is being espoused by these symbols? What parts of the picture are symbols and what parts simply "filler" to enhance the magnificence of the scene?

3. Why do you think that the author uses the term "soon" so often in the last few verses of Revelation? What does this say about the idea that Revelation was written for the "end of the world"?

4. What kind of faith is being presented by the author? Is it a faith that can help persons today? How?

Conclusion

To many persons, the foregoing exposition of the book of Revelation may seem strange indeed. There is no mention of Antichrist, the Second Coming of Jesus, the rapture, the end of the world, nor even a description of heaven. Most of us have been led to believe that the books of Daniel and Revelation contain some mystical secrets which, if properly understood, would give a clue, yea, even a detailed step-by-step analysis, to the mysteries of the end of the world. This has been so much a part of our heritage that it is unthinkable to believe anything else about these enigmatic writings. The simple fact is, however, that neither mentions an Antichrist, nor the end of time, nor a rapture, nor presents a picture of heaven. What both do is to say to people suffering—perhaps to the point of death—under undeserved persecution that God is ultimately the final arbiter in all these matters. What is important is for his people to remain loyal to him in spite of any persecution that will come upon them.

There are great depths of religious insight in this book which definitely become obscured by reading it as a road map for the end of the world. John, along with most apocalyptic writers, spoke as a poet in exaggerated hyperbole! Once we understand this, we can move on to make sense out of this magnificent masterpiece of Christian literature. As with the rest of the biblical writings, the central theme is the supreme majesty and power of God. This concept is exhibited primarily in the visions and in the scenes of multitudes raising their voices as one in hymns of praise and honor to the One who sits upon the throne and to his Lamb! All else that the author attempted to say revolves around that one central theme, but there are a number of other very important sub-themes which need to be emphasized as well.

The most obvious is that of God's justice and righteousness. It is made clear that God's judgment will surely come upon evil in whatever form it appears. Some persons, when they read apocalyptic works, are a bit uneasy, for the writings themselves cry out for the judgment of God to fall upon the evil of the world. There seems to be a far distance between this and Jesus' "Father, forgive them." Yet there is a place for this kind of cry, because the biblical writers all emphasized the serious consequences of rejecting God's laws, his love, and his offers of redemption. The apocalyptic writers spoke to a people sorely oppressed. A modern analogy to this oppression is the Nazi attempt to exterminate the Jews during World War II. Surely if there is any justice in the world and if the God we worship is righteous and just, there must be an appropriate verdict on such hideous evil. *If indeed God's righteousness does not ultimately prevail and such evil does not receive its just deserts, then all of life is a farce, a travesty of law, a jungle in which might makes right and the law of the strong always prevails in spite of any moral considerations!* There definitely is a place in the plan of God for judgment—but it is to be executed by God himself!

This leads to another point. If there is a place for judgment, why is it delayed? Why do God's people have to endure such persecution and suffering? John's answer seems to be that God stays his hand and delays judgment because of his love. He loves all his creatures and desires that all have ample time and opportunity to repent. The cycles which depict partial judgment reflect this motif. The cry of the martyrs, "How long?" is answered with a command for patience. It is not that God does not love his people, especially those who had been faithful to death, but that he loves the enemy also. God's patience and love for sinners led to the gift of his Son and to the death of that Son. The followers of Jesus then cannot expect less than the same treatment which he received. But the great hope is that his suffering can be vicarious, that is, it can lead sinners to an acceptance of the new life offered to all by God.

There is one final aspect that probably needs some fuller explication. This concerns eschatology, the matters connected with the "end." As we have emphasized throughout, the "end" in apocalyptic writing is usually the end of a present age or period of persecution and the beginning of a new age in which the persecution has been removed. When one interprets this as the end of the world, confusion begins to reign. Further, if one attempts to make out of Revelation a chronological history, that effort will be dashed to pieces on any logic that could be applied to the text.

We have for so long viewed the book as a chronological sequence, which gives a step by step historical process by which the end of the world comes, that it seems unthinkable to view the book otherwise. The author seems to be more concerned with making clear several points: (1) evil is to be judged by God, and (2) God's people have a special standing before him. John *never* said that evil would be gone forever (see Revelation 21:27 and 22:14-15) nor that history as we understand it was finished. If, as we read and study the writing, we will attempt to understand the writing as did one of those persons who were undergoing that dreadful persecution, we shall be less likely to make of the book more than it was intended to be. If we can remember also that the book was written in the apocalyptic style and if we would attempt to understand that style as it was intended, more balanced thinking could be secured in interpreting this book.

The book of Revelation is a series of symbols and images which represent certain religious teachings for a people in distress. If we look at the book as a description of how things happen not so much in a chronological sequence but as how they happen *in life at all moments,* we are much more likely to understand the writing. The cycle of the four horsemen, depicting the self-destructive power of a conqueror whose sole purpose it is to conquer, and the cycle of the four trumpets which clearly taught that God directly intervenes to judge evil, are not chronological entities but rather depict certain aspects of the judgment of evil which constantly were and still are at work in this world. It is true that every "age" stands under the judgment of God; it is also true that the Lamb comes in judgment upon the evil of every period of human history, thus destroying extreme evil at certain points and moments. Jesus does "come," but his coming is, as is shown in most apocalyptic works, a return to execute justice on behalf of God's people. This judgment is effective for individuals, groups, or nations, for there is nothing which is outside the jurisdiction of God's sovereignty. These processes of judgment are ever-recurring, ongoing processes just as is God's grace and mercy.

The new Jerusalem is not simply a figure of the future but may always be a present possession where human lives are totally dedicated to God. The binding of Satan for "one thousand years" can occur at any time or place if men and women bind their lives to the Lamb with such an intensity that leads them to witness for Christ even at the risk of giving up their physical existence. What is "Paradise Regained"? It is simply living in the presence of God either here or elsewhere, and this state of affairs can be experienced at any time or place where the believer refuses to worship the beast or to receive its mark.

There are some commentators, however, who do see in Revelation a definite prediction of the "Parousia" of Jesus, that is, his "Second Coming." This is, of course, one interpretation. An interpreter can quite possibly arrive at an entirely different conclusion by studying the book itself. It may well be that the author of Revelation connected the judgment on the evil persecutors of the Christians to Jesus' final coming in order to wrap up all history, but the evidence of the text itself (and of subsequent history) does not seem to point that way. What John the Seer did make crystal clear, however, throughout all the murky symbolism, is that God and the Lamb stand in judgment upon all evil of humankind (Revelation is the only New Testament book that speaks about the "wrath of the Lamb"), especially that which existed at the time of his writing. He emphasized that this evil was temporary and would be destroyed. To read into these symbols a description of the end of the world is to miss John's point completely.

The author of Revelation did not look for the end of the world, but he did look for an end to the persecution. Over and over again he emphasized that these things would take place *soon*. Why, then, did he include such elaborate symbolism and imagery? These figures were used partly because of the type of literature being used to bring the message of hope to the people. They were used because in some small way these gigantic figures could help to demonstrate the significance of what was at stake and what was really going on in the lives of these people. As has been stated previously, John spoke not simply in hyperbole but in exaggerated hyperbole. He did this to make his point. God is sovereign Lord of all creation; evil is an intruder whose existence is very real but whose time is short. God will give those who ally themselves with evil, and there are many, ample time to come to their senses lest they perish with the source of wickedness; but God nevertheless executes his judgment on evil to accomplish his purposes. Through the death of Jesus and his followers, God attempts to show that the power of death and evil is fleeting but that the life committed to God is real and lasting. It was John's conviction that Jesus was already Lord of lords and King of kings and that he would reign forever and ever along with those who committed their lives to him and refused to compromise with the world and its evil. And to that we can all say, Hallelujah, Amen!

Suggestions for Further Study

General Works on Apocalyptic Literature

Hanson, P. D., "Apocalypse, Genre," in *The Interpreter's Dictionary of the Bible,* Supplementary Volume. Edited by Keith Crim et al. Nashville: Abingdon Press, 1976. Pp. 27-28.

Morris, Leon, *Apocalyptic.* Grand Rapids, Michigan: Wm. B. Eerdmans Publishing Co., 1977.

Rist, Martin, "Apocalypticism," in *The Interpreter's Dictionary of the Bible.* Edited by G. A. Buttrick et al, 4 vols. Vol. 1, pp. 157-161. Nashville: Abingdon Press, 1962.

Rowley, Harold Henry, *The Relevance of Apocalyptic.* 3rd edition. New York: Association Press, 1964.

Russell, David S., *The Method and Message of Jewish Apocalyptic.* The Old Testament Library. Philadelphia: The Westminster Press, 1964.

Schmithals, Walther, *The Apocalyptic Movement: Introduction and Interpretation.* Translated by John E. Steely. Nashville: Abingdon Press, 1975.

Commentaries on Revelation

Beckwith, Isbon Thaddeus, *The Apocalypse of John.* Grand Rapids, Michigan: Baker Book House, 1967. (Original edition 1919 by Macmillan Co.).

Even though an older work, this book is exceedingly helpful, especially since the first 197 pages contain a description of apocalyptic literature with a summary of the apocalyptic work known up to that time. It also contains essays on the major themes of the book as well as an exposition and exegesis of Revelation.

Beasley-Murray, G. R., ed., *Revelation.* New Century Bible Series. Greenwood, S.C.: The Attic Press, 1974.

Caird, G. B., *The Revelation of St. John the Divine.* New Testament Commentaries Series. New York: Harper & Row, Publishers, 1966.

Glasson, Thomas F., *The Revelation of John.* New English Bible Commentaries. Cambridge: Cambridge University Press, 1965.

Kiddle, Martin. *The Revelation of John.* Moffatt New Testament Commentary. Naperville, Ill.: Alec R. Allenson, Inc., 1940.

Ladd, George E., *A Commentary on the Book of Revelation of John.* Grand Rapids, Michigan: Wm. B. Eerdmans Publishing Co., 1971. A leading evangelical scholar's view of Revelation.

Morris, Leon, *Commentary on The Revelation of John.* Tyndale Bible Commentaries. Grand Rapids: Wm. B. Eerdmans Publishing Co., 1957.

Commentaries on The Book of Daniel

Brown, Raymond E., *The Book of Daniel.* Pamphlet Bible Series. New York: Paulist Press, 1962.

Hammer, Raymond J., *The Book of Daniel.* Cambridge Bible Commentary on the New English Bible. New York: Cambridge University Press, 1976.

Porteous, Norman W., *Daniel: A Commentary.* Old Testament Library Series. Philadelphia: The Westminster Press, 1965.

77063083R00080

Made in the USA
Columbia, SC
29 September 2019